Mathias Koncen

The Principles of the People's Protection Party

With Schemes, Plans, and Propositions

Mathias Koncen

The Principles of the People's Protection Party
With Schemes, Plans, and Propositions

ISBN/EAN: 9783743687202

Printed in Europe, USA, Canada, Australia, Japan

Cover: Foto ©Suzi / pixelio.de

More available books at **www.hansebooks.com**

THE PRINCIPLES

OF THE

PEOPLE'S PROTECTION PARTY,

WITH

SCHEMES, PLANS, AND PROPOSITIONS.

———————

———————

———————

SAINT LOUIS:
TIMES PRINTING HOUSE, CORNER FIFTH AND CHESTNUT.
1881.

To the Voters of the United States.

In the following pages, I present for your consideration various schemes and propositions, which appear to me as forming a sound basis for the establishment of a new political party. That, in case of their adoption, amendments may be necessary, I will not deny; but the principles embodied are unalterable.

Without authority I present the following named citizens as being best qualified to carry out these schemes, of which they are as yet entirely ignorant—since, to the best of my knowledge and belief, they have never as yet been approached upon this subject—so that the appearance of this book will serve as an introduction both to the author and his work.

The new party may be designated as "THE PEOPLE'S PROTECTION PARTY," with—

FOR PRESIDENT, IN 1884,

JERE S. BLACK, of Pennsylvania.

FOR VICE-PRESIDENT,

BENJAMIN H. BRISTOW, of New York.

And should these gentlemen decline to accept, then I trust that others may be found who will take up the matter.

Very respectfully,

MAT. KONCEN, St. Louis.

April 2, 1881.

SHIP CANALS.

THE NATIONAL BANK SHIP CANAL SCHEME.

It is proposed to apply the money which is now paid as interest upon the bonds held by the Government as security for the National Bank issue, to building ship canals, hereinafter described. Taking as a basis the National Bank circulation of January 1, 1881, which amounted to $343,219,943.00. The Government to issue its own legal tenders for an equivalent amount, with that issue to purchase bonds now held by the treasury as security, thus effecting the retirement of the bank circulation, and abolishing the National Bank system.

The Government should then, for a period of fifty years, apply each year such amount as was formerly required to meet the interest on the outstanding bonds, to the perfecting of the " National Bank Ship Canal Scheme."

The annual interest upon the $343,219,943.00 at 4½ per cent amounts to $15,444,896.00, so that in fifty years, an amount aggregating $772,244,800.00 will have been realized, and should be applied pro rata to the building of the hereinafter-mentioned fifteen canals, or $1,029,659.00 to be applied to each canal per annum.

It is not urged that it would be expedient for the Government to commence, simultaneously, the construction of the whole canal system, but to begin at once upon the *five* which experience teaches would be of greatest benefit to the country. By this latter plan, $3,088,979.00 could be applied to each of the five canals per annum, which, together with such other means as I shall hereafter call attention to, will guarantee the completion of the work in less than ten years.

The river improvement fund should be used for the improvement of rivers from their mouths to the points where the canals will begin.

The following named five (5) canals should be built first, viz :

No. 1.—Hudson River and Lake Ontario via the Mohawk River.

No. 2.—Rock Island and Hennepin via the Old Survey.

No. 3.—Illinois and Michigan via the Old Survey.

No. 4.—Ohio River and Lake Erie via the Wabash and Maumee River.

No. 5.—Michigan City, Fort Wayne and Toledo via Fort Wayne and Maumee River.

The other ten (10) routes are as follows :

No. 6.—Kanawha and James River via The Old Survey.

No. 7.—Rock Island and Green Bay via Rock River, with branch to Milwaukee.

No. 8.—Philadelphia, Rochester, and Lake Ontario via Delaware, Susquehanna, and Genesee Rivers.

No. 9.—Paducah and Mobile via Tennessee and Tombigbee Rivers.

No. 10.—Atlantic and St. Lawrence via Connecticut River.

No. 11.—Mississippi River and Sabine River via Bayou La Fourche.

No. 12.—Portsmouth and Sandusky via Scioto and Sandusky Rivers with branches to Toledo and Cleveland by the most feasible route.

No. 13.—Mississippi and Red River of the North via Minnesota River.

No. 14.—Galveston and Austin via Buffalo Bayou, Brazos, and Colorado Rivers.

No. 15.—Mississippi River and Lake Superior via St. Croix River.

The locks of the above named canals to be 300 feet long, 60 feet in width, and 10 feet deep. The States through which said canals are to pass, to condemn the right of way. The counties bordering said canals paying for property so condemned. Further, that in addition to other labor, the convicts of the States through which canals will pass, are to work on said canals, until they are completed, at the expense of the different States, and finally, the States to relinquish all jurisdiction over canals or navigable rivers to the general Government. No man who has been employed by the Government or by any contractor, 30 days prior to an election, to work on either the canals or improvement of rivers, to be permitted to cast a vote either for President or Governor, or for State or United States Representative.

ADVANTAGES TO BE DERIVED FROM PROPOSED CANALS.

The Illinois and Michigan Canal is too well known to require any comment, but if it is not built, the city of Chicago will be forced to construct a sewer or a canal through the summit level, at her own expense, otherwise the stench will become intolerable during the summer months. If the proposed canal is built, Chicago will rank as one of the healthiest cities in the country, since the lake, being higher than the Illinois River, a strong current will be obtained, and the filth of the city carried away. Moreover, greater depth will be given the river, and larger boats can navigate it. The Illinois River will become a greater feeder for the Mississippi, and vessels can be loaded at Chicago for New Orleans. The advantages of such a water route would be incalculable : for, take the tonnage between St. Louis and New Orleans. A tow-boat successfully manages five barges of one thousand tons each, which would give a gross of five thousands tons per trip, which could be made between Chicago and New Orleans, including delay of discharging cargo at the latter point, inside of 30 days. The one tow of 5,000 tons would be equal to 416 freight cars, or to 13 trains of 30 cars each. The freight upon the tow of 166,666 bushels, at 6 cents per bushel, would be $10,000. The time in transit would be 10 days down and 15 days returning, or 25 days for the round trip, to which should be added 5 days for loading and un- loading. The average daily running expense of such a tow- boat is $200.00, including wharfage and insurance. So that the round trip of 30 days would cost $6,000.00, leaving a net gain of $4,000.00 per trip; that is, provided the return to Chicago should be made without up-freight. Should the tow add one thousand tons in New Orleans for Chicago—say of sugar, molasses, rice or cotton, then $2.50 per ton of freight, or $2,500.00, less $400.00 for additional time (2 days), and deducting $100.00 for extra labor in handling the up-freight and we have the grand net result of one tow—showing gain of $6,000.00. In proof of which, I refer to what has been done by the tow-boat "Port Eads" and others plying between New Orleans and St. Louis, which convey fleets of barges, representing a carrying capacity of 5,000 tons to New Orleans in 7 days, and return from New Orleans to St. Louis in 12 days—at a running expense, as is shown by their books, of $200.00 per day. These barges have transported grain at the rate of 5 1-2 cents per bushel, and there have been 10,465 tons of bulk grain taken from St. Louis to New Orleans in one tow by steamer "Oakland." (See Appendix "C".)

Now with the ship canal built, and the navigation of the river improved, dangers would necessarily be lessened, and the rate of insurance proportionately reduced; while, owing to a permanent and regular depth of channel, the time at present required would be reduced, as greater speed would be possible; and barge lines could carry grain in bulk from Chicago to New Orleans at the rate of 6 1-2 cents per bushel, which would result in a saving to the farmer of about 10 cents per bushel or more than enough to pay his taxes annually. Yet another source of revenue and profit could be created by constructing upon the deck of one barge in each tow a cabin, suitable to the transportation of that class of passengers, known upon Mississippi river boats as "deck passengers." They provide their own provisions and bedding, and can be carried at the rate of $5.00 each either way. Many poor families, desirous of moving, rather than pay $90.00, which is about the rate for a family of four persons, and household goods second-class on railroad, would take the canal and river route at, say, about $30.00, thus saving $60.00—the time lost would be 7 days, but the amount saved per day would be $8.50. The revenue derived from such source would produce a sufficient amount to cover ordinary repairs of boat and barges. Assuming that the tow-boat costs about $45,000 and the barges $5,000 each, then the fleet of tow-boat and five barges represents $70,000, at a profit $6,000 per trip, and a possibility of eight trips per annum, and the net profit would be $48,000 upon the investment of $70,000. Even if the receipts should fall short—say $2,400 or one barge less—the eight trips per annum would yield a profit of $32,000, which we may consider a fair result.

The heaviest losses now experienced upon the Mississippi River are occasioned, outside of stormy weather, by a low stage of water, which causes boats to lay up, owing to their not being able to make the short turns in the channel, and by grounding from one to five days are lost. In order to provide for such contingencies barge lines are compelled to adjust their rates in order to cover losses resulting from stage or condition of the river. Build canals and improve the rivers, and grain can be carried from Chicago to New Orleans at six and one-half cents per bushel, and way-freights—that is, freight for points between New Orleans and Chicago—can be carried by a class of large stern-wheel boats.

The citizens of Peoria contend that to the Chicago sewage is attributable the filthy condition and the terrible smell of the Illinois River opposite to their city. They oppose the cutting of the summit level, in order that Chicago may drain into the Illinois River. But their complaints are unjust. Besides, the well known fact that running water purifies itself, it has been proven by chemical analysis that the water is purified before reaching Peoria. Chillicothe, Lacon, Henry, Hennepin, and Peru, towns located between the end of the canal and Peoria make no complaint. In further proof, if tests are made of water taken from the front of either of the above towns, or from the river in front of the towns of Pekin, Havana, Beardstown, Naples or Hardin, all lying below Peoria, it will be found to be sweet; whereas, an analysis of water taken from the river in front of Peoria, at six different points, lying between one thousand feet above the bridge and four thousand feet below, will prove beyond doubt, that the stench and impurity of the water results from the influx of Peoria sewage, which remains there, as there is not current enough in the river to carry it off. Every steamboatman who has ever visited Peoria, during a low stage of water, is familiar with the fact, that every revolution of the wheel has stirred up from the bottom of the river slimy and offensive matter. Build the canal by cutting through the " Summit Level " and a current will be created in the river, sufficient to carry off the sewage. Whereas, a current of two miles per hour being thus obtained through the ship canal, the water would purify itself, before reaching a point fifty miles from Chicago. As to Peoria, make a uniform width of the river, from half a mile above to the lower end of the city; narrow the channel in front of the city, clean out the slime and filth at the bottom, permit no dumping in front of the town, and, with the proper increase in current, Peoria will enjoy pure water.

The Wabash could be used as a feeder to the Ohio River : as, at its mouth, it is 218 feet below Lake Erie, and the Scioto at Portsmouth is the first river below Pittsburgh, which could be used as a feeder to the Ohio River, it being only 35 feet below Lake Erie when the Ohio is high, and 86 feet below Lake Erie when the Ohio is low. The mouth of the Muskingum is 103 in high water, and in low water 57 feet above Lake Erie.

The Lake Michigan and Lake Superior Ship Canal via White Fish and Train Rivers would be used by lake schooners and propellers. It should be 14 feet deep. A vessel pursuing this route from Chicago or Milwaukee to Duluth would save about 400 miles over the route by the straits of Mackinaw and St. Marie's River, and, in the event of a war with England, the Government could pass her navy from lake to lake without nearing Canada shores.

The Mississippi, Red River of the North Ship Canal via the Minnesota River would not be expensive, from the fact that both rivers head in the same lakes upon the summit of the divide. This latter route completed, then a steamer of 2,500 tons capacity could go from New Orleans to Hudson Bay.

The Rock Island and Hennepin Ship Canal route via Rock River and the Old Survey, with this and other proposed routes completed, then bulk grain could be transported from Rock Island to New York via all water route.

If the Atlantic and St. Lawrance Ship Canal should prove too expensive an undertaking, then the governors of all those States bordering on the Connecticut River to appoint a delegate to a convention, assembled for the purpose of selecting some other route. Said selection to be made with the assistance of a U. S. civil engineer, appointed by the Secretary of War. A decision being arrived at, the same shall be forwarded to the President for approval. Connecticut, Massachusetts, Vermont, and New Hampshire each to appoint three delegates to said convention, and in the event of a tie vote, the United States civil engineer to cast the deciding vote.

The Galveston, Houston and Austin Ship Canal via Buffalo Bayou, the Brazos and Colorado Rivers is a practicable route and a short cut from Buffalo Bayou to Brazos River, and an easy cut from the Brazos to the Colorado River. When the Brazos and Colorado Rivers shall have been improved, by the river improvement fund, to their head waters, then boats can run from Galveston to Houston via

Buffalo Baycu, without going to the Gulf, as the mouths of these rivers afford bad harbors. Galveston favors the cut across from Buffalo Bayou, to say nothing of the fact that a steam ship company, on account of some disagreement with the authorities, has discontinued landing at Galveston, and has constructed a private harbor to the south, which is injurious to Galveston. It is also reported that Jay Gould & Co. have selected the mouth of the Sabine River for the location of a commercial city and railroad centre, since it affords a fine harbor and possesses other advantages that would divert the business of the interior of Texas from Galveston.

BALTIMORE AND ONTARIO SHIP CANAL.

The river improvement fund of the Atlantic Division to improve the Susquehanna from Baltimore to the West Fork —depth of channel to be 10 feet. The convict labor of Maryland and Pennsylvania to be employed upon the work. Extending to where the Philadelphia and Ontario canal passes along the Susquehanna. Counties bordering upon the Baltimore and Ontario Canal to pay for right of way, as upon other canals. It will be advantageous for the State of Maryland to employ her convict labor upon the canal north of the West Fork, although it be out of her territory.

ROCK RIVER AND GREEN BAY CANAL.

This is the only canal that could be utilized as a feeder to the Mississippi River from Lake Michigan, between the mouth of the Illinois River and St. Paul, Minn. At Rock Island the mouth of Rock River is 83 feet below Lake Michigan. At Green Bay, according to Humphrey and Abbott's survey, the mouth of the Wisconsin River is 24 feet above Lake Michigan, and 24 feet below Lake Superior.

The mouth of the St. Croix River is 43 feet above Lake Superior.

MICHIGAN CITY, FORT WAYNE, AND TOLEDO SHIP CANAL.

The Government to construct a ship canal from the most feasible point near Michigan City to Toledo, and improve the Maumee River from Fort Wayne to Toledo. Locks on said canal and river to be 300 feet long, 60 feet wide, and 14 feet deep; and the money designated for the proposed Ohio River and Lake Erie Canal via the Wabash and Maumee Rivers, to be added to the proposed Michigan City, Fort Wayne, and Toledo route, and the two funds would amount to $6,177,958.00 per annum; the convict labor of the State of Indiana to work on said route until completed at the State's expense, and the two above-mentioned routes to be classed as one, and the money to be used to complete the Michigan City, Fort Wayne, and Toledo route first, and then both funds to be used to complete the unfinished part of the Ohio River and Lake Erie route, by constructing a ship canal from Fort Wayne into the Wabash River, and to improve the Wabash River from the end of the canal to Terre Haute, with locks and dams if necessary; the locks from Terre Haute to Fort Wayne to be 300 feet long, 60 feet wide, and 10 feet deep. The funds of the Mississippi River Improvement Division, a fund provided for and hereinafter explained, to be used to improve the Wabash River from its mouth to Terre Haute. The distance by the proposed Michigan City, Fort Wayne, and Toledo Canal route, would be about 500 miles shorter from Chicago to Toledo than via Straits of Mackinaw, and would be open to navigation about two weeks earlier in the spring, and about two weeks later in the fall than the Straits of Mackinaw route, from the fact that it is about 250 miles further south; and with the Michigan peninsula cut-off route completed, and the thirty-two dollars per capita route completed, then a propeller could load at Chicago with bulk grain for New York, Philadelphia, or Baltimore below present rates, and go through direct without reshipping, and have one month longer open navigation annually than by Mackinaw Straits; and also by the proposed routes there would be an outlet for the ports of Lakes Michigan, Superior, Huron, and Erie to New Orleans, via proposed routes and the Wabash, Ohio, and Mississippi Rivers. The master stroke of the proposition is, that the proposed routes will cost the people nothing, except their good will, and therefore 1 vote *yea*.

THE THIRTY-TWO DOLLARS PER CAPITA SHIP CANAL SCHEME.

If Congress should conclude that thirty-two dollars per capita of circulating medium would not endanger the business of the country or cause inflation, then the Government to issue one hundred millions of legal tenders, and with the said issue retire an equivalent amount of outstanding four per cent United States Bonds, applying the annual interest so saved to the construction of the following described ship canals :

The New York, Rochester, Lake Ontario, and Buffalo.

The Philadelphia, Rochester, Lake Ontario, and Buffalo, and

The Baltimore, Rochester, Lake Ontario, and Buffalo ship canal routes.

First, construct a canal from near Newburg, on the Hudson, to the Delaware River; then improve the Delaware to a point most suitable for the purpose of constructing a canal across to the Susquehanna River; then improve the Susquehanna to the West Branch, and to a point most suitable for the construction of a canal across into the Genesee River, and then improve the Genesee River to a point most suitable for the construction of a canal to Buffalo. And if the above thirty-two dollar per capita scheme is adopted, then the New York and Lake Ontario, and the Philadelphia and Lake Ontario Canals, as described in the national bank ship canal scheme, are to be abandoned, and the money that has been designated for said routes to be applied to the proposed thirty-two dollar per capita scheme, which would, in twenty years, amount to $41,186,360.00, and the interest saved from

the one hundred million as proposed by the thirty-two dollar
per capita scheme, would yield, in twenty years, eighty million
dollars, and with the forty million from the national bank
ship canal scheme, would make a grand total of one hundred
and twenty million dollars in twenty years, or six millions
annually; the convict labor of New York, Pennsylvania,
and Maryland to work on the proposed routes until completed at these States' expense.

The River Improvement Fund of the Atlantic Division to
improve the Delaware, Susquehanna and Genesee Rivers
from their mouths to where the canals begin; and at the end
of twenty years, if the three proposed canal routes are not
completed, then the Government to prolong the interest on
the bonds until the proposed canal routes are completed;
and when said canals shall have been finished, then the bonds
shall also be finished, because there will be no principal to
pay. By this scheme we have constructed three ship canal
routes from the ocean to the lakes and have liquidated over
one hundred and fifty million dollars of the national debt,
and at no additional expense to the people.

The depth of the canals and rivers should be 14 feet, since
that would exceed by one-half foot the depth of the Welland
Canal. Vessels can not pass from Lakes Superior and Michigan to Lake Erie drawing over 13 feet, hence it would be
unneccessary to give the canals a greater depth than 14 feet.
Vessels would, upon leaving lake ports, choose this route in
preference to the Welland Canal on account of time and toll
saved.

An American vessel, under existing arrangements, sailing
the Welland Canal, does so under the authority of, and pays
toll to the British Government; and in the event of any
difficulty between the English and American Governments,
the former would at once place an embargo upon the Welland Canal.

With a system of canals, perfected as proposed such contingencies would be avoided, and we could then pass our
merchant vessels or gun boats from the ocean to the lakes

without difficulty. If the uniform depth of 14 feet were to be exceeded, then a larger class of vessels, coming direct from Europe to lake ports would divert commerce from the sea-board. so that cities of the sea-board would find it to their interest to combine to defeat a scheme which could but be attended with injury to them. A 14-foot canal could not do a greater amount of injury to New York, Philadelphia and Baltimore, than the Welland Canal, and the Government should charge all foreign built or foreign registered vessels a tariff of fifty cents per ton—Custom House measurement—the revenue thus derived to be applied to the construction of the Hudson and St. Lawrence Rivers ship canal via Lake Champlain.

The farmers northwest of the canal would save millions annually, on account of cheap transportation; and in the event of war, as before stated, the Government would be independent of the Welland Canal.

The bonds to be bought as proposed by this $32.00 per capita plan, should be four and one-half or five per cent bonds, instead of four per cents, the percentage so gained to be used for, and applied to the construction of the Lake Michigan and Lake Superior ship canal route via White Fish and Train Rivers.

This proposed canal would be a short and not expensive one to cut.

In case the $32.00 per capita route should prove, by survey, to be too expensive, then the money assigned to that route should be employed in making a ship canal of the Erie Canal from Buffalo to Albany, with a branch into the Delaware and Susquehanna Rivers, in order that Philadelphia and Baltimore may have a water route to Lake Erie. The State of New York, by act of its legislature, to donate the Erie Canal and all its franchise to the U. S. Government, and to condemn and pay for all lands, and improvements thereon that may be infringed upon in widening the canal: Provided, however, that all incorporated cities bordering said canal shall, pay for all lands and improvements, which, in their corporate limits may be sacrificed to the enlargement of the canal. Said canal to be a free public waterway, except for a nominal charge upon all vessels, sufficent to keep up, manage, and repair it. The State of New York to relinquish all jurisdiction over said canal to the U. S. Government. All vessels, boats, and barges navigating said canals, to be governed by the same laws imposed upon the navigation of the Mississippi River.

Should there remain any surplus funds after construction of the canals hereinbefore proposed, the said funds to be applied to the construction of a ship canal from the Mississippi River to Lake Superier via the Wisconsin River with branch to Lake Michigan. Such route could be utilized as a feeder to the Mississippi River, since the Wisconsin River at its mouth is 25 feet below Lake Superior; the said surplus to be also used in the construction of the Ohio and Ontario ship canal via Pittsburgh and Rochester, Alleghany, and Genesee Rivers, both of said canals to be constructed and managed in the manner prescribed for the National Bank ship canals.

NATIONAL BANKS.

I now propose to prove that the Government should wind up the national banks, and issue its own legal tenders, in lieu of the circulation thus to be retired, while the interest saved should be used for the construction of the "National Bank ship canals."

The position of the Government is analogous to that of the individual. If a man can show that the receipts from his business are in excess of his expenditures, and that he possesses unincumbered real estate, then the man's note is good, and he can obtain money at a proportionately low rate of interest. According to the report of the Secretary of the Treasury, under date of January 1, 1881, the receipts for the fiscal year exceeded the expenses by $61,441,642.00, and there are millions of acres of land, unincumbered, standing in the name of the Government; hence her note is good, and she is entitled to .enjoy the lowest rate of interest, particularly since her credit is firmly established abroad, and her name has become synonymous with prompt payment; and that at all times she stands ready to protect her creditors. In proof of which statement, I will instance the fact that, when the question arose as to whether the interest on the bonds was to be paid in legal tender or coin (it was understood by the people that it should be paid in legal tenders or lawful money), the bondholders succeeded in having a bill passed through Congress requiring the interest to be paid in coin. As to the manner in which that bill was engineered, I must appeal to the " lobbyists." But the Government, placing a liberal construction upon it, gave the bondholders the " benefit of the doubt," and pays in coin. But that doubt has cost the Government $59,738,000.00, being the amount of premiums paid in nineteen years—that is, from 1861 to 1879.

The Secretary's report to Congress, January 10th, 1880, shows that, from 1861 to 1879, the Government has paid in interest on the public debt, during the past nineteen years, $1,764,256,198.00, which, upon the present population, amounts to $35.18 per capita. The premium of $59,738,-000.00 paid upon gold, amounts to over $1.00 per capita; expense for national loans and currency, $51,523,000.00, over $1.00 per capita—making the total expense to the public, on interest, premiums, commissions, etc., $37.18 per capita; and, taking it as assured, that one-half the debt is owed abroad, and the other half at home, we find that the people have paid for the so-called loyalty at the rate of about $18.60 per capita; and, according to the capitalists' construction of loyalty, lending money to the Government at six per cent is better evidence than the exploits of the laborer, the mechanic, and the farmer, who, leaving his shovel, anvil, plane, and plow, shouldered his musket in defense of the Union. The time has arrived when the Government should say to the gentlemen of the national banks : " Your banks are " to be wound up. Legal tenders will be issued in lieu of " your circulation. You can not object, since you have grown " rich at the expense of the people. At the commencement " of the war you bought my greenbacks with your gold, at a " heavy discount, with the greenbacks so obtained you bought " my bonds also at a discount, and with those bonds you have " operated your national banks." Hence is it not now in order for the Government to abolish the national banking system? Those gentlemen have been well served during the past twenty years, and have become rich off the interest wrested from the people—the bone and sinew of the country. The banks have received their six per cent in gold, but when the Government has called upon the banks for gold, she has been compelled to pay a high premium, although the gold so bought was to meet the next semi-annual install-ment of interest due upon the bonds. Beyond this, the Government has paid banks a commission upon the sales or negotiations of her loans, so that no just grounds of com-plaint can exist when it is proposed to retire the national bank circulation by the substitution of a direct issue from the treasury. The Government has over one million acres of unincumbered lands for every dollar to be issued, and it is time to consider the interests of the people, who for the past twenty years have been groaning under the burden of these interest payments.

It is the people who furnish the men to defend the Union, and not the capitalists. Wind up the banks, and with the interest saved build the national bank ship canals, thus affording employment to the idle labor of the country, and assuring to the farmer, cheaper transportation for his pro-ducts than is promised by the railroad monopolies. By the employment of the convict labor in the heavy cuts, the mechanic will be relieved from the hurtful competition resulting from its employment.

Through fear of inflation the people may demand that the increase of national bank issue be stopped. The present rate of increase points surely to inflation. Moreover, a bill is prepared for presentation to the next Congress to enact a law permitting the present national banks to increase their issue; and should that law pass, then, in a very few years, the issue per capita would reach $32.00, and even higher, unless stopped by Congress, and by that time the Government may have liquidated the national debt, except such bonds as might be held as security for the national bank issue, in which event the banks might petition Congress, through skilled lobbyists, to continue that portion of the debt as represented by them as a "national blessing," so-called.

When the Greenback party started, with its scheme of issue, the bankers all cried out "*Inflation* with an irredeemable paper money;" and so it was, as no limit had been fixed, nor plan for redemption settled upon. The Greenbackers can now cry out *Inflation!* unless the issue of the national banks is stopped. That a certain amount of currency is necessary can not be questioned since there is not enough coin in the world to meet the demands of commerce, but paper money, to have the value of coin, requires substantial backing. If law and power could guarantee to paper the same purchasing power as is possessed by a coin dollar, then the Emperor of Germany, with his half million soldiers and control of the law, through the hirelings of the Upper House, would not permit his Government to suffer, as it does, for want of money. That want of money may be accounted for by considering that the Government lacks stability, that the expenses exceed the revenues, and hence, the value of paper money depreciates.

The United States is at peace with all nations, and at home; her revenue far exceeds her expenses; she possesses millions of acres of unsold lands, ample security for her paper issue; therefore the Government should abolish the National Banks and issue her own *Legal Tenders*. The increased issue, according to the ideas embodied in this work, would gradually run up to the fixed limit of $32.00 per capita, at which point it could be held, until the accomplishment of the objects had in view when it was increased : after that it could be gradually retired as an army officer, however able, no matter how well he has served his country, is retired, when there is no longer any call for his services. The National Banks sprang into being during the dark days of the Republic, but now they are corrupt and arrogant, having outlived their days of usefulness, and, like Lucifer, they may fall, never to' rise again. The National Bank system is, beyond doubt, the best plan ever devised for the protection of a Government that is financially weak—such as was the case with ours at the outbreak of the late war. Thanks to the founder of the National Bank—and thanks to the discoverer of quinine, which though it is a most excellent specific for the ague, we object to taking when we have no ague—as it is bitter. Now, we do not need the National Banks and we object to paying the interest, seeing no reason for the continuance of that expense. The officers of the banks may demand that they (the banks) be continued, simply because they saved the Government from financial ruin at the commencement of the late war; but the Government can answer that, by saying bankers and doctors are alike in one respect —for, when a man is sick, he will call in a physician, take his prescriptions until he gets well : but then he dispenses with the services of the doctor, first having paid his bill, having no further use for him. Now suppose, the physician were to claim, that his patient had done him a great wrong by dismissing him on the ground that, had it not been for his medicines, the patient would have died, and that, justly and out of gratitude, the physician should be retained and permitted to make a daily visit, which should be duly paid for. Would not such a proposition be considered ridiculous? Still the case is similar to that of the Government paying the National Banks for doing things which have become unnecessary. Again, suppose a nurse should call upon one of the bankers and say : "Sir, you have done me a great wrong. "You have discharged me, and that too in the face of the "fact, that had it not been for me and my care, you would "have died during infancy. Hence, I claim that my pay be "continued." The banker would probably respond : "True, "you were indispensable during my infancy, but now I have "no further use for you. Your bills have been paid (if such "be the fact), and you have no just claim upon me." So says the Government to the bankers : "I need you no longer, all "your expenses have been paid, which is a fact, and you "have therefore no just claim upon me." I. have tried to show that doctors, nurses, and the bankers are indispensable appendages to sick men, children, and weak governments, but are useless appendages to healthy matured men and prosperous governments. Hence, if the bankers demand that the Government continue the useless National Banking system, then the Government can justly demand, that those gentlemen retain their useless doctors, pay for their visits, take their quinine for ague, although they have no ague.

Some of my readers may think, that my idea is absurd, but I will suppose another case : That of a man who owns a house and lot of ground, all paid for; he falls ill, is compelled to give up his business or employment, and earns no money for—say one year. His doctor's bills are heavy, but they must be paid, and he finds himself in debt; so he goes to a money lender, and placing a deed of trust upon his property, borrows one thousand dollars for one year at six per cent interest. At the end of the year, having recovered his health and retrieved his fortunes, he wishes to pay off the debt, and release his property from the incumbrance upon it, but the holder of the debt refuses to permit any such arrangement, claiming that the loan should be continued indefinitely, since it had been of so much benefit to the man, while he was in need. Would not that be considered ridiculous? and yet it is no more ridiculous than the action of the National Banks in demanding a continuance of their sway.

RAILROADS.

RAILROADS VERSUS CANALS.

I do not propose to assert that the perfecting of the canal system can do away with the railroads, which I consider the greatest blessings that have fallen to our lot : that is to say, when they are restrained by wise laws. Railroads open up new countries, relieve the cities of their surplus labor, offer employment to thousands of idle hands, and exercise a marked and beneficial influence upon the prices and supply of provisions, and in this way benefit the poorer classes directly. When the crops fail in one section of the country, the railroads can, at low rates, and in a very short time, remedy the deficiency by bringing provisions from those sections of the country which have harvested abundant crops ; again protecting the poorer classes from those high prices, which inevitably follow scarcity. Railroads have answered the purpose better than soldiers, in subduing the Indian, who always retires before the advance of the iron rails. Railroads are the civilizers of the nineteenth century, and do more towards establishing the doctrine of " Peace on earth and good will towards men," than all the so-called ministers of the gospel, who claim to be the followers of Christ and his apostles ; but it is not a fact. Of late years it has become the habit of the clergy of one denomination to ridicule or denounce the followers of other religious doctrines. Some go so far as to denounce as heretics, all those who worship God contrary to their ideas of form or ceremonial, and for this reason their preaching is rather favorable to " war on earth and ill will towards men," than to the doctrine of Christ. Hence I contend that the teachings of the clergy result in more harm than good, for while they preach charity, they *act* in a very different spirit.

That there are good and holy men among the clergy, I admit, and I only allude to those, who, under the garb of religion, and as followers of our Lord, ignore his one great commandment: " Love thy neighbor as thyself." If we are desirous of having others embrace our religious ideas, then we must show by our acts that those ideas are worthy of adoption.

It was a long time before we could introduce our " Pullman Sleepers," those models of comfort, upon the European railways. We sent one over; it was seen, tested, and pronounced good; all the talk in the world could not have accomplished the result of that experiment. It was adopted in those countries. Where government exercises control over the pulpit, no doctrine is permitted save that which teaches loyalty to the crown, as the first great law of Christianity. So long as the clergy obey the dictates of their masters, they are well paid and fed; but let them once question the *divine* right of kings, and they are dismissed. What other inference can be drawn than that such men are unworthy. To such influences may be attributed the birth, in Europe, of those great societies—the Communists and Nihilists,—whose acts have already caused so much apprehension upon the part of the crowned heads. Hence I may state that the influence of the clergy is to keep people apart, while that of the railroad, is to bring them together, and by teaching them each others necessities, to promote good fellowship. The locomotive which Commodore Perry took with him to Japan, did more towards promoting and establishing good will between that empire and the United States, than all the missionaries combined. I am an advocate of religion, since it restrains men from the commission of those acts which are hurtful to society. When Henry VI., King of England, asked as to whether masons were better than other men, he was answered in the quaint language of those early days: " Some masons are not as virtuous as some udher men, but in the most part, they be more good than they would be, if they were not masons." That, is as it reads in a manuscript found by John

Locke in the celebrated Bodleyan Library, and the same remark is equally applicable to religion.

His name is Locomotive—first appearing in England in the nineteenth century. His mission is that of an equalizer of the cost and distributer of the products, and opener of new lands for the over-crowded portions of the earth. He has opened the continents of America and Europe, and ere long will connect Pekin and St. Petersburg, Paris and Rome. Then will the people of all nations come together to trade; they will learn each others ways and religious ideas, from which interchange good must result. The Locomotive may be called the Third Christ, for, like the First, he was received at his advent with shouts of derision, succeeded by cries of welcome and joy. The telegraph may be called his "John the Baptist," who, penetrating the wilderness, tells the people that he is coming—the great Locomotive.

If a President or a member of Congress be guilty of a wrong, it is not the fault of the Constitution. If a Christian do wrong, it is not the fault of the Bible. If a Jew do wrong, it is not the fault of Moses. If a Mason do wrong, it is not the fault of the Order, and if a railway magnate does wrong, it is not the fault of the Locomotive.

As before stated, the railroad brings people from all nations together, people who are necessarily of different temperaments, people whose education and ideas of politics and religion, and whose ways of life are all different; but by association they will, in time, assimilate and learn each others characters. Hence, I affirm that railroads are a great benefit to mankind, but unless they are controlled by wise laws, they may prove a curse, and will oppress the people, by swallowing up, in high tariff, the profit of the farmer, the laborer, and the mechanic, leaving them but a small percentage of their products.

If a man owns a coal mine, iron mines, or valuable quarries, and is compelled to ship by rail, in order to reach a market, it is likely that the railroad company will put on as high a tariff as the freight will stand; but if the miner should stop his shipments on account of the high rates, then the company will make special reduced rates, so as to continue in receiving benefit from the business. Or again, the railway companies by an imposition of high rates, may seek to drive the owners from working their mines, in order that they may send in their agents to purchase them, to be operated for the sole benefit of the corporation. Or again, suppose the price of wheat per bushel is $1.00 in St. Louis and Chicago and the freight to either city from the interior of Kansas is the same—say twelve cents per bushel; now if wheat should advance five cents per bushel in St. Louis, the farmer would wish to ship to that city, in order to derive the benefit of the advance, but the railroad will at once advance the rates of freight two cents per bushel, so that it only benefits the farmer three cents. If a locomotive runs over a farmer's cow, then the farmer has ground for action in the courts for damages against the railroad, on account of the track not being fenced in. But let the railway companies once get control of the Legislatures, and it is only a question of time, unless they are checked in their encroachments in that direction, and the farmer may not only whistle for the value of his cow, but he may even be made liable to the railroad for damages, because he (the farmer) did *not fence in his cow.*

Railroad companies are now required by law to pay county taxes—the same as other residents or resident companies—but once in control of the Legislature, they will probably try to pass an act to exempt railroads from county taxation, on the ground of their being public benefits. Even now it is not an uncommon thing to see accounts in the daily newspapers, of where railroads are striving through the courts to avoid the payment of their county taxes. It is affirmed by the press that the Central Pacific Railroad owns the Legislature of the State of California, and from the nature of the laws and charters that have been passed, the people are warranted in giving credence to the statement.

Will they stop at Legislatures? May they not soon attempt

to control the Government itself, and the judges of the United States Courts and the press? For those who are ambitious will stoop to any act, by means of which the object of their ambition may be obtained. It may occur in the course of time, that a convention of railroad presidents will be called for the purpose of nominating a man for the presidency of the United States, who will obligate himself, if elected, to appoint to office such men as may be recommended by railway managers (see Appendix " D "). With the prosecuting attorneys and judges of the Supreme Court and other courts of the United States in the interest of the great corporations and syndicates, the next step will be a refusal to pay either State, county, or city taxes, and no interference from State Legislatures with their charters will be tolerated.

One would suppose a railroad charter to be a sacred instrument, in that only recently a judge of the St. Louis courts held, that if a charter was granted by the Legislature, the State must protect it, notwithstanding the fact that evidence might be brought forward to prove that such charter had been obtained by fraud. The case was one, in which it was undertaken to prove that a street railroad company's charter had been obtained by fraud—the judge ruling out the evidence on the above grounds. I have no desire to impugn the motives of the judge who so decided, but I do wish to call the attention of the people to the fact, that under that decision a charter is a more sacred instrument than the contract of marriage, for the latter can be set aside and declared null and void, if a fraud be proven. How easy a matter then, to accept the above-mentioned case as a precedent. Should the railroad party succeed in electing a President, you may expect to see judges appointed, who will be in the interest of the railroads, and Congress will be powerless. The judges of the Supreme Court pass upon the constitutionality of laws, and the President, the army, and the navy are sworn to support and sustain the Constitution, and the laws of the United States as decided by the Supreme Court. So that it will be an easy matter for the railroads to ride over the will of the people.

Can we recall to mind any act, upon the part of the great railway corporations, that should be viewed with distrust and alarm by the people? I think we can. During the Chicago convention, it was publicly announced by the press that "Jay Gould" was on his way thither, accompanied by Blaine and delegates, to beat Grant. When Gould found it impossible to nominate Blaine, he, being a railroad man and faster than a soldier, switched off to a side track during a recess, hitched his Blaine delegates to Mr. Garfield, and pulled him through the convention, to the infinite disgust and chagrin of the " Third Termers."

As to the influence of railroads over judges of the United States courts see Appendix " D." See what the New York correspondent of the *Detroit Free Press* has to say concerning the action of Conkling, in a suit of the Pennsylvania Railroad Company, pending in the U. S. Court, for the recovery of $500,000.00 taxes paid under protest.

I shall now endeavor to inventory and point out the power of these great corporations, show what they may effect by combining with the party in power, or independent of that party, how they can nominate and elect their own man; for a campaign fund of $25,000,000.00 and one-ninth of the popular vote is not a bad nucleus. In the meantime the people are supposed to be, and are, ignorant of the fact that they are voting for a railroad candidate.

On the first day of January, 1881, there were 93,898 miles of completed railroad in the United States and Territories, according to the *Chicago Railway Age*, and the number of men employed on the roads per mile was eleven, according to the report of the railroad commissioner of Illinois to the Legislature of that State, under date of January 15th, 1881. According to this, there are 1,032,878 men in the employ of the railways, and an assessment of $25.00 per man would yield a fund of $25,821,950.00 for campaign purposes; this statement does not include street railways, which may be counted upon for co-operation. In the civil service of the United States Government there are

100,000 men, who have been assessed at an average of $25.00 per man, by which means a campaign fund of $2,500,000.00 was realized ; so that with the Government and the railroads —irrespective of the street car companies—a campaign fund of $28,321,950.00 can be raised.   As the $25.00 assessment is usually begun about twelve months previous to an election, — and is payable in installments, they find it cheaper to pay than to resist.   The number of railway and civil service employees is 1,132,878 ; and as the popular vote of 1880 was 9,192,595, it is seen that the railway and civil service, or pool vote, was fully one-ninth of it.   Little could be said in praise of the managers of a party, if, with a campaign fund of twenty eight million dollars, and one-ninth of the popular vote fully assured to them, they were unable to elect the man of their party.   When this is considered, it is easy to calculate the enormous strength of the party in power, which can only be broken by electing a President for six, instead of four years, who is to serve but one term, and who can never be eligible for re-election to the same office.   Let him retire to private life upon a pension of $10,000.00 per annum, to continue during his life, or that of his widow. This will be an inducement for the president to discharge the duties of his office honorably ; and will obviate the necessity of his being compelled to sign fraudulent railroad charters, in order that he may secure a competency for his children, in the shape of *presents of stock* in the companies working under these fraudulent charters.

Let us adopt the river improvement and the ship canal schemes ; and, above all, let us use our energies to preserve the integrity of the judiciary.   We must look to the courts for means to defeat the illegal acts of presidents, congressmen, governors, and legislators.   An act passed by a Legislature, or by Congress, for the benefit of the few, and to the injury of the people, may be repealed ; but the decisions of the Supreme Court, be they in the interest of the people or in that of the great companies, must stand, and the President, with the army and navy, is sworn to support them, and the people are without redress. The people have no one but themselves to blame, if these things come to pass, because their representatives are supposed to represent them truly. The people, since the war, have been truly represented, for they have been corrupt, and their representatives, in order to truly represent their constituents, have been compelled to be corrupt also. Hence the people have no ground of complaint. If the people desire a change, let them first change themselves. Let them substitute vigilance for indifference, reason and christian charity for blind prejudice, and honesty for corruption, then they will be more careful in the selection of those men who are to fill the public offices. Railroad companies claim that they only desire to realize eight per cent upon the cost of their lines, and to prove it, they show the cost of the road, its expense, and receipts. This is done in order to convince the people that present rates are necessary in order to accomplish that result (see Appendix "C"). The people may decline to pay those rates, affirming themselves to be willing to pay such rates as will net the present owners eight per cent upon their investment, but not upon those portions of the roads that were built at the expense of the people or the Government. The Government donated public lands to some roads, and the inhabitants of counties, and cities, and towns donated right of way and money. Cities and counties have taken stock, and the managers have worked it in such a manner, that the roads, being sold out under first mortgages, were bought in by the managers, who used for that purpose the earnings of the roads; in other words, these managers succeeded in managing the people out of their stock, and now own the roads, at about one-half the original cost, and the people are expected to pay interest upon that very money out of which they have been swindled.

Reliable railroad magazines have undertaken to show the entire cost of the different lines, and the interest has been based upon these reports. It is now in order for some one else to demonstrate what the railroads cost their present owners; what the interest at eight per cent will be, and then the people will realize the difference. To begin with, let us consider the Pacific railroads, what tariff it is necessary to impose upon their travel, in order to net the investors eight per cent. The 42d Congress appointed a committee, who made careful enquiry into the cost of the Pacific railroads, and the report was as follows:

" First.—We find, not one dollar was ever risked in the payment of stock subscribed to, which was required by law to be paid. Second.—We find that the whole cost of construction was, in round numbers, $50,000,000. Third.—The companies received $54,000,000.00 in bonds or $4,000,000.00 more than enough to build and equip the road. Fourth.— We find a stock and bonded account amounting to upwards of $113,000,000.00, or a profit to the companies of about $63,000,000.00 above the cost of construction. Hence—

Received Bonds from the Government.....$	54,000,000 00
Received from sale of Stock and Bonds....	113,000,000 00
Received from sale of Donated Lands up to February, 1881...............	36,000,000 00
Land not sold, $43,000,000 acres, at $2.50 per acre.....................	107,500,000 00
Total.................... $	310,500,000 00
Deduct whole cost of Roads.............	50,000,000 00

Gain to present owners—The Road and.... $260,000,000 00 which amounts to an assessment of $5.18 per capita of present population. The English Government has never bestowed a pension upon any of her privileged class, that can compare with the amount given these Pacific railroad gentry So, whither are we drifting?

The $63,000,000.00, over and above the cost of the Road, as represented in the bonded indebtedness of $113,000,-000.00, can not be viewed in the light of a legitimate debt due by the road; since it is in excess of the cost and equipment, but it was necessary for some one to hold the first mortgage, in order to bar the Government's second lien, and therefore, with the earnings of the road, they, the managers, notwithstanding the fact that they were the officials of the roads, sold to themselves as private parties, the first mortgage bonds. It may be thought that in the near future, other roads entering California and San Francisco will have the effect to break down the monopoly that has been enjoyed for so long a time by the Central Pacific; but this is not the case, for the latter road controls San Francisco, as the "Turk does Jerusalem," and as all Christians entering that city pay tribute to the Turk, so will no person be able to enter San Francisco without paying toll to the Central Pacific. Stanford & Co. control all the railroads entering San Francisco, as well as nearly all the steamships and city railways.

The cost of the Iron Mountain Railroad from St. Louis to Pilot Knob was nearly $4,000,000.00. It was sold by the State for $1,350,000.00.

The Missouri Pacific cost over $6,000,000.00 and was sold by the State for $3,500,000.00 and so on, all over the country and the people were inevitably the losers; hence, the people object to paying interest upon money that they have virtually lost; but they are willing to pay 8 per cent on such amounts as the roads have actually cost the present owners. The Government should, therefore, establish rates on the Pacific Road from Omaha to San Francisco, on a basis of $60,000,000.00 as the cost of the road.

RIVERS.

RIVER IMPROVEMENT SCHEME.

The total amount of money in circulation on the first day of January, 1881, was $1,321,552,797.00, or $26.35 per capita. According to the "London Economist," of January,

1879, France had a circulation of $27.37 1-2 per capita; and we think that this country with its enormous business, could safely increase its circulation $5.65 per capita in excess of France without incurring danger from inflation.

It would require an additional issue of $183,023,703.00 to increase our per capita rate from $26.35 to $30.00 per capita. Therefore let the Government issue this amount, and retire a similar amount of five per cent bonds, and with the interest saved upon these bonds, improve the rivers of the country.

The interest saved would amount annually to $9,151,-185.00 which should be divided into three equal parts of $3,050,393.00 each, and if those bonds were to run 50 years, the interest would amount to $457,559,450.00 and that again would be divided into three equal parts of $152,519,816.00 each. Then separate or class the rivers under three grand divisions: The Mississippi Valley Division, Pacific Division, and the Atlantic Division, to each of which would be applied annually as above stated the sum of $3,050,393.00 for providing rivers with permanent banks, and building locks and dams for slack water navigation, if necessary—it being understood that the main rivers of each division are to receive attention, first:—say the Mississippi from New Orleans to Alton, Ill.; then the Ohio from Cairo to Pittsburg; next the Mississippi, from Alton to St. Paul; then the Missouri from its mouth to Sioux City; next Red River from its mouth to the North Fork; then the Arkansas from its mouth to Wichita, Kansas; and next the Cumberland to Nashville, and the Tennessee to Florence, Ala. The same plan should be pursued in each division, so that the most important parts of the main rivers may be improved first; and when that has been done, go back and complete the improvement to the headwaters of each river. If it be found necessary to construct dams and locks, the Government to exact the amount of toll necessary to keep the same in repair, and cover the expense of management. If, at the expiration of fifty years, the system of improvement has not been fully completed, then the Government should make further application of the interest accruing from the retired bonds.

Such a system could not be a burden upon the people ; it would furnish employment to thousands of idle hands, and not only this, but future generations would derive the benefit resulting from cheap transportation, and, at the same time, it would act as a wholesome check upon railroad monopolies.

I will enumerate the rivers to constitute the three divisions :

The Mississippi Valley division to consist of all rivers that flow into or out of either the Mississippi and its tributaries, the Sabine River and its tributaries.   .

The Pacific division to consist of all rivers that flow into the Pacific Ocean, and Gulf of California, and also to include the Texas streams, not otherwise mentioned.

The Atlantic division to embrace all rivers not tributary to, and East of the Mississippi.

INFLATION.

Such a scheme would do away with much sectional strife, and would relieve Congress of the continued wrangles over river appropriations. Of course, the national banks and their henchmen will oppose this scheme, upon the ground of the danger of inflation, just as they opposed the Greenback party a year ago. They were right in opposing that party, because, according to their doctrine, there was no fixed limit to the issue of paper money, and as a matter of course, that would be attended with disaster. But this scheme provides for an issue of only $32.00 per capita. Still it would be opposed by the national banks, as it conflicts with their interests. Every resolution that has been offered in Congress, looking towards the issue of a fixed amount of **Legal Tenders** for the purpose of buying up United States bonds has been opposed.

According to the Comptroller's report of January 1st, 1881,

I will show that the national banks do not restrain their acts from fear of inflation, for the increase of National Bank currency for the past year amounted to $2,258,727.00, and fifty nine new banks were organized with an authorized capital of $7,673,066.00, so that one would not infer that the banks fear inflation. When the national banks issue paper money they call it *furnishing currency for commercial transactions,* but when the Government issues paper money they call it INFLATION; which is a distinction without a difference. To illustrate: the wife of a plebeian is in need of some kind of garment which her husband is too poor to purchase; in order to obtain it, she resorts to shop-lifting; she is caught in the act, arrested, prosecuted, convicted, and condemned to imprisonment for *stealing,* notwithstanding that her husband has offered to pay the shopkeeper for the stolen goods. Now the wife of a rich banker commits a similar offense. She is arrested and tried, according to law; the pleading is, that it is not a clear case of theft (as her husband is rich), it is ascribed to mental derangement, and it is called by the name of *"kleptomania,"* and the lady is discharged, and her husband pays for the stolen goods—the difference between kleptomania and theft is, that one is *greed* and the other *need.* So, for the Government to issue Legal Tenders, it is called inflation, but for the National Banks to do *identically* the same thing, it is called supplying the country with currency.

So long as the circulating medium is kept within the limit of $32.00 per capita, there is no danger of inflation. As before stated, France has $27.37 1-2 and England has even more. Fix the limit at $32.00 by act of Congress, and make the Legal Tenders receivable for all private and public debts, except the interest on the bonded debt, which is payable in coin, also make them receivable to the extent of fifty per cent of duties on imports. To begin the year 1881 with National Bank issue, General Grant & Co. organized a national bank in New York, with an authorized capital of $3,000,000.00 and no complaint of *inflation.* But had the Government wanted to issue $3,000,000.00 of Legal Tenders to buy up and destroy the same amount of United States bonds, then the 2095 national banks, that are now in operation, the officers thereof most likely, would have held an indignation meeting and cried out *inflation.* These men were raised as pets, and the people are asked to indulge them in their hobbies.

I will now close the prosecution of the national banks, and will submit the case to the voters of the United States, for their consideration, together with the following propositions:

First.—There are at present about 2100 national banks in operation, with an issue of $350,000,000.00, and they have on deposit with the Comptroller of the Currency about $385,000,000.00 worth of United States bonds, drawing on an average 4 1-2 per cent interest annually, which amounts to $17,375,000.00, and allowing twenty men to each bank, and that would aggregate 42,000 men engaged in the National Bank business. The population of the United States, based upon the census of 1880, was 50,152,550; and now the question is, whether it is more prudent for the Government to tax 50,110,550 of her citizens to the amount of $17,375,000.00 annually to pay 42,000 of her privileged class citizens to do that, which the Government can do herself, or to wind up the national banks and issue her own Legal Tenders in lieu thereof, and thus save $17,375,000.00 annually; and the interest, so saved annually, to be expended for the construction of the proposed national bank ship canals.

A republic is for the benefit of the majority.

A monarchy is for the benefit of the minority.

And therefore, to strengthen a republic, it is necessary to weaken the chartered monopolies and privileged class gentry. Now, Mr. Voter, you are a juryman in this case, and are requested to hand in your verdict at the next presidential election, and before presenting your ballot, acquaint yourself with this fact: That the tax of the country is principally collected from *men,* directly or indirectly, because women and minor children seldom pay taxes. Therefore, the voters are the tax payers, and as there were, at the last presidential election, 9,192,595 voters, now divide the $17,375,000.00 that is annually paid to national banks as interest on their bonds, by the number of voters of the United States, and the result will be $1.89 for each voter; and then, before dropping your ballot, ask yourself this question : Shall I vote for the Government to give my proportion of the said $17,-375,000.00 annually to a privileged class gentry to spend in enjoyments at Saratoga, Long Branch, etc., etc., or shall I vote for the Government to use the said $17,375,000.00 annually in constructing the proposed national bank ship canals, and thereby give employment to the idle labor of the country, furnish cheap transportation to the farmer and manufacturer, and be an offset to railroad monopoly ; that ballot will help decide whose funeral this will be.

RIVER IMPROVEMENTS.

LAND GRANT SHIP CANAL AND RIVER IMPROVE-MENT SCHEME.

Provided, that in those States where the following canals are to be constructed, and river improvements instituted ; the United States Government or States shall donate from the public lands, a strip five miles wide upon each side of the rivers, extending from their mouths to their head waters. In case such lands have been already taken up along those rivers, then an equivalent quantity to be donated in some other section of the State.

This scheme is to embrace all States west of the Mississippi River, and northeast of the Mississippi above St. Paul, Minnesota, to Lake Superior. The funds acquired from the sale of those donated lands, in connection with the funds derived from the $30.00 per capita plan, designated in the

Mississippi and Pacific Divisions of the River Improvement
plan, to be applied to improving the rivers from their mouths
to their head waters.   When it becomes necessary to build a
ship canal, in order to connect two rivers, then the Government shall donate strips of land ten miles wide upon each
side of 75 miles below the head waters of each river, including the divide between the two rivers, and the money derived
from the sale of these lands is to be applied to building the
canal, which is to begin twenty-five miles below the head
waters of each river.

The River Improvement Fund of the Mississippi and
Pacific Divisions to be applied to improving those rivers to
point of beginning of the canals.   Convict labor, of the
States or Territories to be benefited, to work upon the canals
at the expense of the several States.   None of the donated
lands upon these routes to be sold to any one, except to
actual settlers.   The land to be sold at $2.50 per acre, and
the titles or letters patent, to be withheld until such settlers
have resided upon said lands for five successive years, and
they shall pay for the lands when the deeds are granted.
If a man settles upon a tract of land—and he shall in no case
enter more than a quarter section, or 160 acres—he shall
have the right to sell out to some other settler, and the latter
shall receive credit for the time during which the former
occupied the land.   The settlers upon these lands shall, after
a residence of three years, pay an annual assessment of five
cents per acre, towards the construction of canals; such
yearly payments to continue until the completion of the
work.

If other portions of these lands shall be devoted to other
purposes than farming or grazing, then five cents per front
foot, of lots 300 feet or less in depth, shall be collected
towards defraying the cost of canal construction.

Each State, wherein the proposed rivers and canals are to
be improved or constructed, is to relinquish to the general Government, all jurisdiction over the routes which are to be public
highways, and subjected to the same laws and regulations as

govern the Mississippi River; the Government to charge lockage for passing through the canals, but only an amount sufficient to cover cost of management and repairs. In case valuable deposits of mineral be found, during the excavations, the Government is to reserve the right of working them for the benefit of the canal construction. There shall be a roadway, at least 50 feet wide, upon at least one bank of the river or canal, running parallel to it, and extending its entire length; said roadway to be built and kept in repair by the counties bordering upon the route. If any State, wherein a proposed canal is to be constructed, or a river to be improved, refuses to comply with any or all the above conditions, then the Government shall refuse to improve rivers of the said State with money obtained from the $30.00 per capita plan. Furthermore, in addition to that strip of land 5 miles wide, a strip one-half mile in width, running parallel to that donation, should be set aside in common, in order that trees, where there are none, may be planted, and a belt of woodland thus be perpetuated, from which not only the settlers, but the face of the country, would derive incalculable benefit. These strips of woodland need not necessarily be placed along the outer boundary lines of the 5 mile donation, but had better extend through their centers, either equi-distant, or say one-half mile upon the one side and one and a half miles upon the other, from the water lines. If these schemes appear to be worthy of adoption, U. S. civil engineers should be detailed to survey the several routes, and if the money provided by the several methods herein specified should be found insufficient, then donate more land, or construct a Ship Railway upon Capt. James B. Eads' plan. It would be much more simple, and certainly less expensive, to construct a railway adapted to the transportation of river steamers, than for ocean going steamers or sailing vessels, as the latter are narrow and top-heavy, requiring very strong tracks and cradles in order to insure steadiness; while river steamboats are flat-bottomed and *not* top-heavy. The class of boats that would be most likely to run upon said rivers and canals, would be stern-wheelers, such as now ply upon the Ohio River.

Take the steamer " Montana," for example, her dimensions are as follows : 250 feet long, 48 feet beam, depth of hold 5 feet, carries 1,300 tons, drawing 6 feet of water. The "Montana," weighs about 600 tons, while a steamship, of a like capacity, weighs about 1,000 tons. So it is evident that it will cost much less to build a ship railway for river boats, than for either ocean steamers or sailing vessels ; so that if it is not practicable to build ship canals in order to connect rivers, why build ship railways?

I will now propose

" THE FORT BENTON AND WALLA WALLA SHIP CANAL ROUTE. "

The Government to donate strips of land 10 miles wide upon each side, from Fort Benton on the Missouri River, to Walla Walla on the Columbia River, including the divide between the two rivers. Assume the distance to be 1,000 miles, that would give 12,800 acres per mile, which is the exact amount that the Central Pacific Railroad and the Oregon Railroad received per mile for over 350 miles of road; that would be in money, at the rate of $2.50 per acre, $32,000.00 per mile, and the 5 cents per acre tax $640.00 per mile. The total land grant for the distance would be 12,800,000 acres, which at $2.50 per acre would aggregate $32,000,-000.00. The 5 cent per acre tax would yield $640,000.00 per annum, or $19,200,000.00 in 30 years. The 5 cent per foot on town lots, would about offset those lands not taken up. It should take 30 years to complete the routes, for it would be unwise upon the part of the Government to rush public works that would afford employment to so many men. The available convict labor of Washington, Idaho, and Montana Territories, amounts at present to about 600, and it is safe to anticipate an annual increase.

So soon as $1,000,000.00 shall have been accumulated from the sale of donated lands, and the tax of 5 cents per acre, the Government should commence the system of improvements, beginning with the Missouri and Columbia

Rivers from Fort Benton and Walla Walla, the point of beginning of the canal; convict labor to be employed upon the main cut through the mountains. The entire route from Walla Walla to Fort Benton, to be classed as one canal route. The initial work upon this route will attract attention, induce immigration, and the donated lands will soon be taken up.

The head waters of the Missouri and Columbia, are about 30 miles distant from each other; a man standing upon the top of the mountain divide being able to see both rivers. The class of boats best adapted to this route, is similar to those plying between New Orleans and Cincinnati, i. e., stern-wheelers, 300 feet long, 45 feet wide, 7 or 8 feet depth of hold, total width, including guards 50 feet, height from keel to top of officers cabin—called "Texas"—45 feet. It would be necessary for these boats to lower their chimneys and remove their pilot-houses, in order to pass through the canal-cut tunnel. They could be towed through by a "tug" cheaper and more rapidly than they could make the run with their own power, since they could not, of themselves, attain a rate of speed sufficient to insure steerageway; they would be continually bumping against the rocky walls of the canal, which could but be attended with diminution of speed, and serious injury to the boats themselves. The canal-cut tunnel would be 50 feet wide, and 45 feet in altitude, which is an immense hole to work through solid rock, as it would be nearly 20 miles in length. During the course of 30 years, however, the convict labor of these Territories could drill a hole of great extent through solid rock.

It is fair to estimate $20,000,000.00, as the cost of improving the rivers with locks and dams, to insure a 10-foot gauge for slack-water navigation from Fort Benton to Walla Walla, to head waters at canal cut. A residue of $12,000,000.00, and $640,000.00 per annum from the 5 cent per acre tax, would remain for the canal cut. The time has arrived when the convict labor of this country should be employed upon public improvements, for the benefit of the people, instead of being employed by private contractors for manufacturing purposes, which latter course works to the disadvantage and positive injury of the honest laboring classes, who are forced into competition with it.

If after the canal-cut tunnel has been completed, it should be found necessary to enlarge it, the work could be done during the winter months, when the rivers are frozen over, by letting out the water. A bed or space might also be cut for the accommodation of a railway track, to be used by any company who would guarantee to the Government, such pay for the use of it as Congress would adjudge to be equitable and just. The revenue thus accruing to be applied to the repair and improvement account of the canal and rivers.

Railroad companies should not be prevented from constructing a road from Fort Benton to Walla Walla on line with the canal and river, in order to facilitate transportation during the winter season, when the rivers are frozen over.

CONVICT LABOR.

To return to convict labor—there are at present, in the States and Territories, over 50,000 convicts, which number is being increased daily. If the plan of leasing them to private contractors, engaged in manufacturing, be persisted in, what, is it reasonable to suppose, will be the condition of the honest mechanic, in ten or fifteen years? By that time, the number of convicts may be estimated at about 100,000, exclusive of the inmates of workhouses, or houses of correction and of refuge, and the damage to the honest mechanic, by the introduction of this volume of cheap penal labor into the manufacturing field, is beyond computation. A protective tariff, is only in the interest of the private contractor, and there will remain but one way by which the honest mechanic can procure food. He can breakfast upon the vote which he has cast in favor of a party who furnishes him a "spread-eagle" speech on protective tariff; for dinner, it may fill his stomach with gas, and give him the amount of courage requisite to running around hunting up honest jobs, which he may not find ; but he may find a policeman, who will arrest him as a suspicious character, and upon the charge of having no visible means of support, he may be sentenced to the workhouse, where he will receive food, and as a convict, work for the private contractor. O, wise laws!—I do not assert that convict labor will monopolize the manufacturing interests of the country, but I do assert, that it may absorb that interest to such an extent, that it will compel manufacturers, who employ other labor, to reduce their scale of wages, in order that they may enter into successful competition with the product of convict labor. Furthermore, it is only a question of time, and we will see rolling mills in full operation at the penitentiaries. Hence, I advocate the employment of convict labor upon public works, ship canals, etc., leaving the manufactories to the honest working man, who will, in that case, see some benefit accrue to himself from a protective tariff, which in the other event, as far as his interests are concerned, had as well be consigned to the devil at once.

PUBLIC LANDS.

When the Government is solicited to donate her lands for the construction of canals and the improvement of river navigation, it can in no wise, be considered in the light of asking that public lands be given to private parties or corporations, as in the case of the Pacific Railroads. Lands were not only donated to those roads, but $64,000,000.00 in the shape of bonds. In addition to the 181,000,000

acres of land given to the Pacific Railroads, they have a
claim on 61,907,000 acres more. On January 1st, 1881,
they owed the Government, principal and interest, the sum
of $79,994,572.00, which they are refusing to pay. If the
Government can afford to give 181,000,000.00 acres of the
best land, and $64,000,000.00 in money to the Pacific Rail-
ways, to say nothing of the millions of acres donated to
other railroads and private parties, it certainly can not object
to donate lands, with a view toward the improvement of rivers
and the construction of a canal system. The case is similar
to that of a man using his money for the purpose of improving his own property for his own benefit.

In petitioning the Government to donate these lands of the
people, it should be borne in mind, that they are not given
away for nothing, for they are to be sold, and the money
obtained is to be used for the benefit of the people. Whereas,
in the case of the railroads, no equivalent has been received.

If these River and Canal schemes are not adopted, then, in
the course of time, all of the public lands will have been
disposed of, the money spent, and nothing will remain to
show for it. The Pacific Railroads have received to date,
from the sale of public lands, $36,000,000.00.

CANALS.

The Walla Walla and Fort Yuma Ship Canal Route via
Lewis, Snake, and Green Rivers, Salt and Utah Lakes, and
the Colorado River. Government or State to donate lands
15 miles wide, upon each side of said route, subject to the
same conditions as those governing the donations to the
Walla Walla and Fort Benton Route.

The Sioux City and Red River of the North Ship Canal
Route, via Big Sioux River, Yellow Bank and Minnesota
Rivers. Government to donate lands 10 miles wide upon each
side, from the mouth of the Big Sioux, to the Red River
of the North. This, and other lands, donated for the purpose
of constructing routes hereinafter set forth, to be subject to
the same conditions as those governing the Walla Walla and
Fort Benton Route.

Des Moines City and Red River of the North Ship Canal Route, via the Des Moines, Wontonwan, and Minnesota Rivers. Government to donate lands 10 miles wide upon each side of said route.

James River and Sheyenne River Ship Canal Route, via James River, Dakota Territory. Government to donate lands 10 miles wide upon each side, from the mouth of the James River to Sheyenne River, opposite Devil's Lake, to improve the river and build a canal.

James River and Sheyenne River Ship Canal Route, via Fort Ransom Reservation. Government to donate lands 15 miles wide on each side of said route. A 25-mile canal will connect the two rivers, and that will give an outlet to the Red River of the North, into the Missouri River at Yankton, Dakota Territory.

Colorado and Rio Grande River Ship Canal Route, via Gila or San Juan and Charmer Rivers, or via the Rio Chaco and Puerto. Government to donate lands 20 miles wide upon each side of the route, from the Colorado River to the Rio Grande.

Minnesota Lakes Combination Canal Route—surveys to be made, and the most practicable system selected. Government to donate lands 10 miles wide upon each side of all rivers and lakes that may be considered a desirable route for commerce.

Mississippi River and Lake of the Woods Canal Route, via Sandy Lake, Savannah Creek, St. Louis River, Vermillion Lake, Vermillion River, Rainy Lake and Rainy Lake River. Government to donate lands 10 miles wide upon each side of said route, in order to improve the rivers and lakes, and build canals to connect with the Mississippi River and Lake of the Woods.

If a surplus should exist from any of the formerly mentioned proposed canals, then the said funds should be used to construct a ship canal from the Mississippi River to Lake Superior via Wisconsin River, with branch to Lake Michigan. This route could be utilized as a feeder to the Mississippi River, since the Wisconsin River at its mouth is 25 feet below Lake Superior; said surplus also to be used for the construction of the Ohio and Ontario ship canal route via Pittsburgh and Rochester, Alleghany and Genesee Rivers, the above two routes to be constructed and managed in the manner provided for the national bank ship canals.

FREMONT'S DRY LAKE SCHEME.

Government to donate 1,500,000 acres of the public lands, to improve Dry Lake, as per proposed plan of Gen. John C. Fremont.

San Francisco, Sacramento and Columbia River Ship Canal Route, via Upper Sacramento River to North Fork, and canal to Goose Lake, then canal into South Fork of Asparagus River, thence into the East Fork of Des Chutes River, thence to the Columbia River. Government or State to donate lands 15 miles wide upon each side, from the North Fork of the Sacramento River to the Columbia River.

Willamette River Ship Canal Route. Government or State to donate lands 10 miles wide upon each side of the river, from its mouth; connection to be made with the Sacramento and Columbia River Route.

Missouri and Rio Grande River Ship Canal Route, via the Yellowstone and Powder Rivers, and canal to North and South Platte, via Blue River, then along South Platte to Beaver Creek, thence by canal into Duck Creek, then to Arkansas River, connecting the Arkansas with the Canadian River by canal, via Los Animos river, and connecting the Canadian with the Pecos River by canal. The Government and the State of Texas, to donate lands 15 miles wide on each side of said route, from the mouth of the Yellowstone, to the mouth of the Pecos River.

"The Missouri and Rio Grande," "The Fort Yuma and Columbia River," and "The Colorado and Rio Grande River" Ship Canal Routes, can not be completed for many years to come—possibly not during our day—but the Government should survey and locate the routes, and designate the lands that are to be donated for these improvements. The money derived from the sale of those lands, to be invested in State bonds, which should be held by the Secretary of the Treasury of the United States, until a sufficient amount having been accumulated from the sales of land, and interest on the bonds so purchased, it would justify the commencement of the work. The above named canals, will afford an unlimited water-power for manufacturing purposes, and thus enable the manufacturers to pay their employes living wages, and at the same time, enter into successful competition with foreign manufacturers, who being burdened with the heavy expense incidental to costly motive power, are compelled to scale their wages down. If the Sauk and St. Louis Rivers in Minnesota, were improved by slack water locks and dams, they could also furnish motive power to an unlimited number of factories.

Minneapolis and Red River of the North Ship Canal Route, via the Mississippi River, Lake Itaska, wild Rice River or Red Lake River. Government to donate lands 15 miles wide upon each side, from Minneapolis to the Red River of the North.

RED RIVER OF THE NORTH.

The Government to donate lands 10 miles wide upon each side from the line of the British possessions, to the head waters of the Minnesota River. One fourth of said lands to be applied to the Mississippi and Red River of the North Ship Canal Fund, or the Minnesota and Red River of the North, to be classed as one route.

Lake Superior and Mississippi River Ship Canal, via Fond du Lac, St. Louis and other rivers. Government to donate lands 15 miles wide upon each side, from Fond du Lac, to the Mississippi River. By completing this route, the manufacturing interests of Minnesota will derive considerable impetus from the great water-power thus afforded. An outlet from Lake Superior to Hudson Bay, Pacific Ocean, and Gulf of Mexico, will be obtained by the completion of the routes hereinbefore and those hereinafter to be mentioned.

Kansas City, Topeka and Denver Ship Canal Route, via the Kansas, Republican, and Platte Rivers. Government to donate lands 15 miles wide upon each side of said route, from Topeka to Denver. If this route is completed and the Mississippi and Missouri Rivers are improved, then the farmers of the States of Colorado, Nebraska, and Kansas, along said route, could ship grain by barge to New Orleans, at about 8 cents per bushel; such being the case, the agriculturists along this route could well afford to pay the annual tax of 5 cents per acre, because they would save at least 10 cents per bushel on their grain, by cheap transportation the result of the proposed routes, and that would be an eqivalent of about $2.00 per acre, and this scheme only asks 5 cents per acre.

The Missouri and Red River of the North Ship Canal Route, via Goose and Cheyenne Rivers, thence to Missouri River, at some point between Bismarck and Fort Stevenson. Government to donate lands 20 miles wide upon each side of the proposed route, from the Missouri to the Red River of the North, reserving a strip one-quarter of a mile in width, parallel to, and back one and one-half to three miles from the canal or river—this reserve to be held in common forever—as timber and grazing land for the benefit of the occupants of the donation. If the reserve is found to be bare of timber, then trees should be planted, first at the expense of the River and Canal Fund, applied to that route, and kept up in Dakota by that fund, until the Territory becomes a State and counties are organized, when the county courts will take charge of the strip, and keep it planted with timber at the expense of the occupants of the donated lands.

It should not be forgotten that the Northern Pacific Railroad, near and in a parallel line to the proposed ship canal, received from the Government as a free gift 50,000,000 acres of the public lands. If no difficulty is experienced in

·obtaining an adequate supply of water for the proposed canal, it·will greatly benefit Northern Dakota, for in that section there is great scarcity of wood and water, on account of which three crops out of five fail. The timber would increase the rain fall and the canal would irrigate the soil. In order to drive the Indians from Dakota, let the President issue a proclamation, setting forth that any hostile Indians found within the Territory will be sentenced to ten years labor upon the canals. If such a course does not drive them away, the compulsory labor may civilize them.

The Red River and Rio Grande Ship Canal Route, via the Big Wichita to the Rio Grande or to the Pecos River, the line to be east of the headwaters of the Brazos and Colorado Rivers. The State of Texas to donate lands 15 miles in width, on both sides of the route, from the mouth of the Big Wichita on Red River to the end of the route, and to set aside a strip of land one-half mile wide—same as the Red River of the North and Missouri River Canal—the object of which is identical with that of this latter proposed route.

Galveston Bay and Red River Ship Canal, via Trinity River. Texas to donate lands 10 miles wide on each side of said river from the mouth of the Trinity River to Red River. The canal to be built from fifty miles below the head waters of the Trinity to Red River. The River Improvement Fund of the Pacific Division to be used for improving the Trinity River from its mouth to the proposed canal.

It is not intended to convey the idea that the ship canals should be located just as the routes are herein designated, but surveys should be made in order to determine the most practicable route. Texas values immigration more than she does her lands, and the proposed ship canal and improvements of rivers will encourage people to buy the lands. As a proof that Texas is liberal with her lands, she offered a fixed amount of public lands per mile to any company that would build railroads in the State, and she offered 3,000,000 acres to any one that would build a State House—such as would be accepted by the Legislature; and

the Canal and River Improvement scheme would enrich the
State as much as a railroad.

The proposed ship canal schemes ask the donation of public lands for the public good, and all the acres asked for
will only about balance the number which have been already
granted to railroads. For every canal that is herein proposed, there is a subsidized railroad on a parallel line near
to it. The railroads are in possession of the choice lands,
because they located their lines through the fertile valleys,
in order to get choice lands, for they very well knew that in
the course of time the money derived from the sale of land
would more than amount to the original cost of the road.
The Pacific railroads have received already $36,000,000.00
from the sales of land, and still they are not satisfied, but
are evidently trying to have men, who are in the railroad
interest, appointed as Judges of United States courts ; Judges
who will hold local taxes to be illegal. As the law is now
executed, a person might think that Congress and the Legislatures have a right to condemn private property for private
benefit and public injury.

The people locating on the canal lands could even afford
to pay the annual tax of five cents per acre toward the completion of the routes, as it would take 35 years for the payments to reach the cost of the lands of the Pacific railroads,
as the average price obtained by them for lands sold is $4.25
per acre.

The River Improvement and Canal schemes should therefore be adopted, as they can not be a *monopoly.* The Government, the States, the counties, and the people that are to
locate upon the donated lands, can afford what has been
asked herein, since the money will be expended along the
proposed routes, and will fully compensate the givers. The
scheme creates the wealth with which to complete itself.

The reader may think that the construction of the proposed canals will involve too great an expense upon the present population of the United States, but it is not so great an
undertaking, in proportion to the present population of the

United States, as it was for the people' of the States of
Indiana, Ohio, New York, and Pennsylvania, to build about
two thousand miles of the DeWitt-Clinton canals about
forty years ago. The citizens of the above named States had
to stand a heavy taxation to meet the expense of the construction of State canals, whereas the citizens of the United
States do not have to submit to an increase in taxation to meet the expense of constructing the proposed
National Bank and Land Donation Ship Canals ; and further,
the cost per capita of the present population of the United
States would not be so great for the construction of the
proposed canals, as the cost per capita was for the people of
the above named States to construct their two thousand miles
of DeWitt-Clinton canals forty years ago. Therefore the
Government should at once survey, locate, and begin the
proposed ship canals and stick to it like a Jesuit until the
object had in view is accomplished, and thereby improve
nature's natural transportation routes.

DAKOTA TERRITORY DAMMING SCHEME.

The people of Dakota Territory say that the prairie lands
are not worth a d—n, but *I* say, that by building dams they
will be worth a d—n. Any one familiar with Dakota, is
aware that during the summer months, there is but a slight
rainfall in that region. This may be attributed to many
causes. The snow falls during the winter, and is blown
by the high winds into the valleys, so that when the spring
thaw sets in, the water rans off at once from these snow reservoirs, and the Missouri River, being unequal to the influx
of so great a volume of water, overflows its banks. Now
this accumulation in the valleys of the snow from the hills
and mountains, necessarily deprives the face of the country
of one great source from which to derive its rainfall, as the
distribution of these snows over a large extent of country
would be more favorable to evaporation. As it is, the rapidly melting snow flows out before there is time for evaporation. By building dams across the lower ends of many of

the valleys, natural basins would be formed, wherein the drift snow would be retained, so that when the spring thaw sets in, large bodies of water would remain thus imprisoned, from which a continual evaporation would necessarily insure a greater rainfall, and the hitherto arid plains would become valuable and fertile. Still another great advantage to be derived from such a system, would be the possibility of controlling the Missouri River, and preventing those disastrous inundations for which it is noted. There are many streams in Dakota, which, being dependent upon the thaws for their supply of water, are dry two months after the first thaw. By damming these streams at intervals, from their mouths to their sources, they would also be transformed into great natural reservoirs. Without this system, Dakota can never become a farming country, for at present, three crops out of five fail, on account of the drouths, but in some portions of the Territory, *three* crops *out of two* fail; that is, a farmer and his family will strive to make a living on some of the land, but his crop fails the first year; if it fails the second year, he and his children most likely starve, which makes three failures. The proposed remedy is for the Government to donate lands five miles wide upon each side of all the rivers and creeks that run dry and such valleys as may be selected for reservoirs or water basins. The money received from the sale of lands to be used in the construction of dams. The Government should also plant a strip with timber one-half mile wide running parallel to the basins, rivers, and creeks. The Government should also donate one section of land near the centre of each township in Dakota and all other Territories and States where the Government owns lands, to be used as timber lands and to be held as such in common by the townships forever.

THE NON-FORFEITABLE HOMESTEAD BILL.

The States to enact a law, whereby any person desirous of obtaining a lifetime homestead, may procure a dwelling house and lot, the same to be registered in a book kept for that purpose by each county in a State. The book to be known as the "Homestead Register." The lifetime homestead being duly recorded, shall be exempt from all legal execution. Tax shall not be levied except upon the value of the ground. The buildings to be declared exempt so long . as they are used as dwelling houses, or for purposes connected with dwelling houses, but if any building or buildings or part thereof be used in conducting any business of profit whatever, then the tax to be levied as the law directs with respect to business premises. The mere keeping of an office, however, by a resident family not to be considered as conclusive that the same is being used for other purposes than as a dwelling.

Any lifetime homestead having been duly recorded as such, the owner to be prevented by law from selling or disposing of the same. A homestead in a city or town to be limited to the extent of one block or less. A homestead to be devoted to the pursuit of either farming or grazing, to be limited in extent to one hundred acres or less. A homestead for orchard or vineyard to consist of fifty acres or less.

Any person owning a homestead who may wish to remove to some other locality, or to some other State, can do so, by applying to the Judge of the Probate Court of his county, and if it can be shown to the satisfaction of that official, that he has purchased another homestead, that it is clear of debt, and worth at least two-thirds of the value of the present homestead, then the Judge shall issue an order permitting the sale at the owner's will. But if the new homestead that has been purchased is not clear of debt, then the Judge shall appoint the Public Administrator as trustee for the sale of the present homestead, the proceeds thereof to be applied to liquidate the debt on the new homestead, and the balance, if any, to be turned over to the owner, less the trustee's costs and commission. The object of a trustee is to prevent a man from depriving his family of the benefit of his homestead. A homestead once recorded, can never be lost, which is an inducement to every right feeling man, and as the main foundation of orderly society is to have peace at home, therefore one must first obtain a *home.* If a man is deprived of or loses his money, he becomes a coward, for he will then submit to insult and imposition, that he would not submit to if he had money.

If every newly married couple would procure a homestead, the evils resulting from loss of home and support would be lessened.

In the majority of families, when the *necessary* money is "*non est,*" then the *unnecessary* devil is to pay. Preachers may preach, preach on to eternity, but they can not restore peace and harmony to *that* family. Patience will cease to be a virtue, the wife will become soured and sullen in disposition ; the children neglected, will forget obedience ; the husband, desponding, will lose courage, and by neglecting the discipline of his family, fail in his duty, and what is the result? It is from such houses as I have just painted, that the criminal ranks are recruited. This homestead law would relieve society of much of this evil, and the State can well afford to lose the homestead tax, as it will be more than made up in the amount saved by having a less number of criminals in her penitentiaries and jails, dependent upon her for support. As a man is under no obligation to get a family, having once gotten one, he is under obligations to provide for its support; so the State, while it has no right to compel a man to get a family, does have the right to compel that man to support his family, when he has got it, so as to prevent that family from falling, in the end, upon the State for support. A man should have no more right to dispose of his homestead than he has to dispose of his family. A creditor should have no more right to take a man's homestead for debt, than he should have to take the man's family ; and the State should say to the man : "If you will be prudent enough to obtain a homestead for your family, I, in turn, will be prudent enough to protect you in its possession." It shall not be obligatory upon a man to live upon his homestead, because some men, having built large dwellings, might meet reverses, which would compel them to curtail their expenses, iu which case, they could rent a less expensive house which would be paid by the lease of their homesteads. Even now, many men would build large, fine dwelling houses, but the high tax levied deters them from so doing.

VOTERS.

Congress to enact a law to the effect, that all men connected with the civil service shall not be entitled to vote for either President, Vice-President, or Member of Congress. Such a law would only place them in the same political position as the citizens of the District of Columbia. All of those Government officials, who have, directly or indirectly, the power of either employing or dismissing men who are in the service of the Government, should, before being permitted to enter upon their official duties, be required to make oath that they will not, either directly or indirectly, . cause assessments to be levied for " campaign purposes " upon those who are under their official control. Such a provision would sensibly curtail the strength of the party in power, and save the civil service man his earnings. The same law should apply to all officers of chartered or licensed companies, corporations, or institutions that employ men; it should also require those officers to make oath that no undue influence shall be exercised to control the votes of their employees.

Such laws would operate as a protection to the mechanic and laborer, and as a check upon political corruption; and those parties who, by the aid of the earnings of their employees, seek to advance their corrupt political designs.

COAST HARBOR SCHEME.

Should it be deemed wise to adopt the " National Bank Ship Canal Scheme," the " River Improvement," the " $30.00 per capita," or the " $32.00 per capita Schemes," two per cent per capita should be added annually in order to keep pace with the increase of population.

The population of 1880 was over 50,000,000, therefore the Government should issue one million of Legal Tenders annually, buying up therewith four per cent bonds. The interest saved upon those bonds would be $40,000.00 per annum, and since one million in bonds would be retired annually, the interest saved would amount to $2,120,000.00 in ten years, to $8,120,000.00 in twenty years, to $18,060-000.00 in thirty years, and to $31,860,000.00 in forty years.

The interest so saved should be used for the improvement of coast harbors. If this scheme is adopted, the Government will, in forty years, have reduced the national debt $40,000,000.00, whereas, if this scheme is not adopted, the people will have to pay the forty millions of bonds and interest to private parties.

Galveston harbor to be improved first. If the circulation is increased to a basis of $32.00 per capita, that amount, together with the extra million issued annually to keep pace with the increase of population, will wipe out about one-half of the present national debt, or $768,219,943.00, and the danger of inflation would not be nearly so great as apprehended; from the fact, that the increase per capita would be gradual, it would take several years to wind up the national banks, and for Congress to shape the proposed schemes. Furthermore, the one million to be issued annually to keep pace with the increase in population is not quite two per cent. The loss upon paper circulation, resulting from various causes—fires, etc.—is about one-sixth of one per cent; so from such causes the $32.00 per capita circulation would suffer a shrinkage of over one and one-half million dollars per annum: hence there can be no inflation so long as the Government restricts the circulation to within $32.00 per capita. By the proposed schemes the national debt would be reduced to about eight hundred million dollars, for which the Government would have to provide; and as there is a surplus of nearly $60,000,000.00 annually over and above ordinary expenses (see Report for 1880), then $50,000,000.00 can be applied annually to the liquidation of the national debt, and in sixteen years the Government would be free from debt. The $10,000,000.00 of the unapplied annual surplus should be used to purchase coin, with which again to retire an equivalent amount of Legal Tenders, and in forty years about one-half of the total amount of Legal Tenders will have been retired, and coin will gradually become the money of the Republic. In addition to the $60,000,000.00 surplus mentioned heretofore, another surplus will accrue from the amount of interest saved every year upon the bonds purchased as proposed with the $50,000,000.00—two millions additional per annum would be saved in this way, and one million of this amount should be expended per annum in constructing fortifications for coast defence. In sixteen years $55,500,-000.00 will have been expended, and such disbursements of money in various parts of the country for coast defenses and other public improvements would also lessen the dangers of inflation, from the fact, that it would keep a large number of men employed annually, and thereby keep money in motion. The Government should not buy up bonds exclusively in New York City, as it might cause inflation in that metropolis; but in order to guard against such dangers, the Government should purchase bonds at different times, and at different places. The other half of the interest saved from the last mentioned surplus should be set aside, each year, by the Government, as a war fund, which should be held in reserve until it amounts to $100,000,000.00, so that, in the event of war, the Government would not be at the mercy of money lenders, as she was during the late civil war. The best fortification that a Government can build against an enemy is a *money fund;* then the army can be handled. Without money, the money lenders will handle the Government, as they did at the commencement of the last war; when they exacted forty per cent premium for gold.

In order to keep said fund from remaining idle, it would be well to apply three-fourths to the purchase of the bonds of such foreign Governments as appear most likely to get into trouble with this country; then, in the event of war, the United States Government, by the sale of all of the foreign bonds on hand to the bankers of the country with which war seemed imminent, the power of the enemy would be much weakened, financially.

When the war fund shall have reached the fixed limit of one hundred millions, the surplus accruing annually, should be devoted by the Government to the construction of new, and the improvement of old, coast defences.

HOME BOND BILL SCHEME.

The Government to guarantee the bonds of the States, counties, and cities, upon the following conditions; each State to enact a law, accepting these conditions:

First.—That the President of the United States appoint a commissioner, to be known as the "Home Bond Commissioner"—he to hold office during a term of six years, and to receive a salary of $8,000.00 per annum, with additional allowance for clerk hire. The duty of the commissioner and his clerks shall be to keep a correct account of the total assessments levied in each State, county, and city. Congress to prescribe the amount of indebtedness which a State, county, or city may incur; which should be limited to—say twenty per cent of the total assessed valuation. If any State, county, or city wishes to borrow money for the purpose of refunding their bonded or other debts, then a certificate shall be filed with the Home Bond Commissioner at Washington City, showing the total assessment of said State, county, or city; said certificate to be sworn to by the Auditor, Comptroller, Assessor, and two members of each Central Committee of each political party. Upon presentation of the said certificate to the said commissioner, bonds shall be issued to said State, county, or city, to the extent of the limit fixed by act of Congress. The bonds shall be signed by the Secretary of the Treasury of the United States, and by the commissioner, who shall keep a record of all bonds so issued, in a book kept for that purpose, which shall be open to public inspection, and the Treasurer and Comptroller of State, county, or city shall also sign the bonds.

In case a State, county, or city, shall default, either in interest or principal, then the U. S. Treasurer shall pay the said delinquent, interest or principal out of funds not otherwise appropriated, the President to appoint a collector for the said delinquent State, county, or city, the collector's office in each being taken possession of by a U. S. Marshal. The taxes collected shall be applied to the payment of the debt assumed by the Government, as well as all expenses attending the collection. All bonds so issued, shall be payable, both principal and interest, at the main commercial city of the State for which the said bonds were issued. All expenses incurred by the Home Bond Commissioner at Washington, D. C., such as salaries, stationery, printing of bonds, etc., shall be paid by the States, counties, and cities, in proportion to the bonds issued to them.

By this scheme States, counties, and cities could fund all their debts at a lower rate of interest than at present, because their creditors would be safe, as they would be protected by the General Government, the same as the holder of a national bank bill. The holder of a note does not regard the State, county, or city from which it is issued, so long as the Government is held; and just so it would be with the Government guaranteed bonds. The bonds should be of uniform size and printed upon the same kind of paper. As these bonds could be deposited as collateral security for nearly their face value, it would enable persons holding them to transact business to a better advantage than with the present State, county, or city bonds, as they bear different rates of interest, ranging from four to ten per cent, and their value ranges from par to seventy-five cents discount. The Home Bond Bill bonds to draw interest at the rate of four and one-half per cent per annum, payable semi-annually, one-half in *coin* and one-half in Legal Tenders. The principal to be payable in the same manner. The bonds to be called " five-fifties "—the maker having the right, after the expiration of five years, to call them at option. The said bonds to be exempt from all taxes. The States would gain by the low interest and no tax; for at present the States, counties, and cities loose the tax on bonds, as they are held by parties who can not be reached by the assessor; and the proof of this fact is, that the assessor's books of any State, county, or city will show, that there is not one-fifth of the bonds that are outstanding returned for taxation. By the present plan, the States pay from four to ten per cent interest on their bonds, and count on getting some of that back in the shape of taxes. So the State does not get the tax, but, nevertheless, she pays the interest, whereas, by this scheme, the tax would be collected in advance, by reason of the lower rate of interest.

The farmer and manufacturer can say : " I can now invest my money with safety, since I have no fear of being over-taxed on account of the increase of the State debt, as there is a limit fixed by law." A sinking fund should be created in each State, county, or city, to meet the bonds, and it should be—say five per cent per annum of the gross revenue.

In case any county, having a less amount of indebtedness than the limit, wishes to issue more bonds, it can be put to the vote of the people. The money so raised to be used for purchasing timber land in each township, to be held in common forever, under the control of the County Court. (See Appendix " G.")

A county can also buy ponds, lakes, and creeks, that may be suitable for reservoirs or fish hatcheries; the same to be improved and stocked.

A State, county, or city, may have a larger debt than the fixed limit, in which case, bonds may be issued to fund the over-debt; but for the liquidation of that over-debt, a separate sinking fund should be created—such bonds to run 10 years, and to be known as "two-tens." (See Appendix " H.")

COMMISSIONS CLAIMED.

It should be understood and agreed, that in the event of the United States Government adopting the " National Bank Ship Canal Scheme," or the " River Improvement Scheme," herein proposed, that a commission of 5 cents per capita, on the basis of the census of 1880, shall be paid to me, as the originator of said schemes.   I have a clearer case in equity to claim a commission for a scheme that will liquidate nearly one-half the present national debt, without increasing additional taxation or debt, than the syndicate has to claim a commission for negotiating a national loan, that will but perpetuate a debt upon the people.

It is shown by the Secretary's report to Congress, January 10th, 1880, that the Government has paid for expense of national loans and currency, from 1861 to 1879, over $51,-000,000.00, and therefore, I claim the said commission. Notwithstanding that the Government may make amendments to the schemes ; that is to say, if the main feature of the " National Bank Ship Canal Scheme," and the " River Improvement Scheme," as herein proposed, are the bases of any plans the Government may adopt, then the said commissions are to be paid to me ; payable in annual installments during ten years, commencing from the date of the passage of the said bill.

It should also be agreed and understood, that in the event of one or more States adopting the " Home Bond Bill," as herein proposed, I may claim from said State or States two thousand dollars each, as a commission for introducing said bill, the said two thousand dollars to be paid to me, within six months after the passage of said " Bond Bill."

Any amendments to said bill, not to invalidate my claim to the commission ; that is to say, if the main features of the scheme, as herein proposed, are the basis of any bill that any State may adopt.

STATE RAILROAD REGU-
LATIONS.

Twelve commissioners to serve in each State, two to be appointed by the Governor; two each to be selected by the Senate and House of Representatives, and six to be elected by the popular vote. The duty of the commissioners shall be to examine books and all other evidences, in order that the actual cost of all railways, to their present owners, may be ascertained. Said commissioners are to be vested with the power to send for persons and papers, to employ expert accountants, or such other clerical help as may be necessary. A thorough examination to be made into the expenses and receipts, and the amount of business done during the past three years; the average result of one year will thus be ascertained, and from that average, can be based such traffic and passenger rates as will yield a net surplus, which should be a fair profit upon the cost of the roads to their present owners. The rates having been fixed, they should be submitted to the legislature for approval.

The salary, and term of office of said commissioners, to be fixed by the State, which shall pay the same for that period consumed in ascertaining the present status of the different roads; after that, to be paid by the railroads, and to be accounted for as part of the operating expense of the road. The result would justify the means, for the roads and stock would be kept in better order, the officers and clerks would be better paid, and the trackmen and brakesmen, who now receive but forty dollars per month, would most likely be advanced to fifty or sixty dollars per month. On the Cleveland, Columbus, Cincinnati and Indianapolis, and on the Indianapolis and St. Louis railroads, these forty dollars per month trackmen and brakesmen, who are in constant danger, are compelled to sign the following certificate, which is known and called by the signers a " Death Warrant;" it will be found on page 11, under Rule 12, of a publication issued by authority of the roads, and reads as follows : " The regular compensation to employees, covers all risks or liabilities to accidents." Men, who prefer to suffer such an imposition, rather than starve, or take to the highways as tramps, may also submit to being told by the managers, as to whom they shall vote for President of the United States ; and they may also submit to an assessment for a campaign fund. As I have shown that the total pooled railroad vote was over one-ninth of the popular vote in 1880, it is to the interest of the employees, to favor this and other measures herein mentioned. If the managers find that the business of the roads increases, they will, most likely, say to themselves, that rather than lower the rates they will apply the surplus earnings to the improvement of the roads and their equipment, and raising the pay of all hands on the roads and thereby the community at large would be greatly benefited, as the roads and their equipment would be kept in better order ; and hence, danger to life and property materially lessened. The commissioners are to meet but once in three years, and the rates, then established by them, shall hold for three years. There should‘ be at least four old commissioners upon every new commission. The object in having twelve commissioners is, that being selected in four different ways, it is a guarantee to the people that there will be a correct investigation of railroad affairs, and a correct report to the Legislature. Whereas, as the law now stands, for one or three commissioners, and they appointed by one man, it is an easy thing for one of them, if he be corrupt, to make the position worth, at the expense of the people, about double that of the President of the United States. If any railroad manager or director should conspire to defraud the stockholders, or, by false entries, to cause an untrue exhibit of gain, and it can be proven before the proper court, he should be prohibited from holding any office in any chartered corporation.

CONTROVERSY IN "UNCLE SAM'S' FAMILY.

I propose, in what follows, to represent the Government as *pater familias*, the States as sons, cities as daughters, counties as grandsons, and the territories as those children who have not yet reached their majority. When the father obtained his divorce from his wife, mother England, the children followed his fortunes. The estate was divided and the thirteen sons received each a portion. In consideration of the youth of the minors, the father acts as guardian until they become of age, and are capable of assuming control of their property and domestic affairs.

In consideration of the various complications likely to arise, concerning the postal service, money matters, commerce, foreign treaties, army and navy, tariffs, inter-state commerce, and the rights of citizenship, the thirteen brothers agreed that it was to their mutual advantage to employ the "old man" as their attorney in fact, for the performance of certain things duly set forth in a written instrument known as the "Constitution of the United States of America;" he, the "old man," to make solemn oath, that he would faithfully abide by the said Constitution, all things not embodied therein to be left to the management of the brothers. If, in the course of time, it was found necessary to increase or curtail the power thus conferred upon the "old man," the brothers to exercise that prerogative, provided a three fourths' vote of all the sons that were of age, was taken or cast in its favor.

The "old man," like a good many other men, who have taken advantage of the law of divorce, finally became very dissipated and reckless, so much so, that the boys became jealous of each other. One insisted upon it that "Cotton was King," another conferred upon "Hay" that proud distinction, and so on. The "old man" strove to quiet and pacify them, by the administration of soothing syrups, labeled "the Dred Scott decision," "Mason and Dickson's Line," "Squatter Sovereignty Bills," and "Helpers' Impending Crisis," but without effect, other than to inflame, to a greater degree, the minds of the unruly boys who, finally, from words, came to blows. As Napoleon once observed, "the Lord is always on the side of the heaviest artillery," it is unnecessary to state which side was triumphant, but the triumphant side will long remember what a fight it had. The "king" question having been arbitrated out of existence by the sword, the boys met at a grand centennial celebration, holden at the city of Philadelphia, and then and there agreed to make friends and forget. In straightening up affairs, they found themselves not only without money but heavily in debt; so after discussing the matter they concluded to effect some arrangement with the "old man." With that in view, the grandsons (counties), the daughters (cities), with the old boys (States) bringing up the rear, wait upon the "old man." Jackson county is delegated to begin the interview That county arrives in due time at the White House, salutes the "old man," tells him of his debts, and begs that he guarantee his bonds. The "old man" says: "Why do you not have your father, Missouri, guarantee your bonds?" Jackson: "That would not appreciate their value. I ask *you* to do it, as it would enable me to fund my debt at a much less rate of interest; to secure you in the transaction, I will bind myself to fix a limit beyond which I can not increase my indebtedness, say 20 per centum of the total assessed valuation of all my property, so that you will have no trouble caused by my not being able to meet principal and interest." "Old man": Well, Jackson, my boy, how did you happen to become so heavily involved?" Jackson: "Grandpa, in this way: I loaned money to railroads and took their stock, out of which they swindled me." Old man: "Jackson, I have been watching some of you boys, and I think you have committed many mistakes, so I will give you lecture number one. I hope that you will profit by it in the future."

"First—You should learn the dodge of railroad tricks, and know that a dozen men can form a company, with, say $100,-000, get a charter through the Legislature, pay your county newspapers to advocate the road, give a little stock to the most influential persons along the line of the proposed road in order to induce the people and towns to grant right of way, depot grounds, and money to the railroad. Otherwise the route may be changed in order to pass through a town favorably and liberally disposed. They also make it to the interest of your county Judges to order elections, when the people vote to make the donations or to subscribe stock, by such means and schemes, and with their original capital of $100,000.00 they manage to grade the road; then, to complete it, money is borrowed upon first mortgage bonds. The earnings of the road are first applied to the repayment of the $100,000, and afterwards to the purchase of the majority of the first mortgage bonds. That course is persisted in until the stockholders begin to make trouble, and then they sell the road under the first mortgage lien, by which plan, they wipe out *all* the first stockholders. You are lucky if you get your taxes, and although the original stockholders may not be as rich as they were, still they have drunk from the cup of experience. My second lecture is to the effect, that you do not give the Judges of either the county or criminal courts the power of appointing Grand Jurors who are the safeguards of the people against political corruption. Suppose that the central committee of a political party meet in caucus and select one of their friends as a candidate for Judge of either the county or the criminal court, that by fraud, he is counted in, that he knows it, consents to it, and takes his seat; then suppose that some one of the committee commit some fraud, either in connection with the county treasury, or in election returns, and he is brought before the Judge, what kind of decision might be expected? Why, sir, a man might as well sue the devil in a court holden in hell."

These corrupt Judges, who have the power of appointing Grand Jurors, fear but two things—the small pox and the U. S. Marshal; the former, because it is impossible to have that case continued *indefinitely*, and the latter, because he is apt to bring them before some Court, wherein neither the Grand nor Petit Jury are creatures of his own, to explain why the county has so large a debt; and hence he fears that Court.

To what is to be attributed the fact, that there are so many criminals at large? It is to a great extent the fault of the Judges and the Prosecuting Attorneys, who are altogether too liberal in granting continuances, to say nothing of their occasionally being criminals themselves. You have neglected to watch the Prosecuting Attorney, in order to prevent his making a charge a degree higher or lower than the evidence will sustain, so that the cases are dismissed on account of flaws in the indictments. You have neglected to look after the Judges, in order to prevent their making illegal rulings, in order that their friends might have new trials upon the ground of illegal rulings of the Courts, and thereby wear out the prosecuting witnesses. You have neglected to scrutinize your jury lists, so as to make certain all men are legal jurors, and to prevent the swearing in of illegal jurymen, for the purpose of hanging the jury in place of the murderer. I suggest that you frame a law, so that nine jurymen be sufficient to acquit or convict. Christ, in selecting his apostles, got one Judas, and we, who are not nearly so good judges of men, may concede three out of every twelve men to be Iscariots. Guard against these possible tricks of corrupt officials, as it may lessen crime, the criminals knowing that they can not trifle with the Courts.

As to your public schools, take warning from Washington's farewell address. Show no partiality to foreign nations. I say, apply the same to your public schools. Show no partiality for foreign languages; do away with the dessert, and introduce substantial food, in the shape of the gymnasium. Teach the boys military tactics, and encourage them to turn out on the Fourth of July, so that the present generation may grow up imbued with the same patriotic idea as animated the souls of the past, and then in case of war, the Government can recruit a well drilled army in a short time. Make it as a qualification for holding office, that a man shall have attended public school for at least three years, and a foreigner who, when he arrived here, was under seven years of age, should be subjected to the same rule. So Jackson, my boy, adopt these suggestions as to your school system, guard your school expenditures, or the growling tax-payers and the intriguing Jesuits may succeed in abolishing the entire system, through corrupt legislation. Adopt and embody these principals in your State Constitution, and when you shall have rectified these errors which I have pointed out, then I will guarantee your bonds."

DAUGHTER CINCINNATI'S PETITION.

Sisters Cincinnati, Orleans, Memphis, and others hold a convention for the purpose of devising ways and means to overcome their financial embarrassments, and they conclude to send Sister Cincinnati to the " old man" to state their grievances, and implore assistance. Cincinnati arrives at the White House, and is welcomed by the "old man."

Old Man.—" Why, daughter, you appear to be in trouble ; how is it that you are dressed in mourning? Has any one of the family died?"

Cincinnati.—"Yes, poor Sister Memphis is dead."

O. M.—" Poor Girl! Of what did she die?"

C.—" Of a most disgraceful and contagious disease, one that finds many victims among those cities who are hopelessly in debt. The bondholders call it the 'Receiver's Plague,' and some of my sisters already complain of premonitory symptoms, so they have sent me to you for a remedy."

O. M.—" Memphis, poor girl, has been sorely afflicted ; a gunboat fight going on in her front, Federals and Confederates fighting to the north, east, and south of her, and herself a victim of the yellow fever : she passed through all to die of the ' Receiver's Plague '."

C.—"Yes, father, and I am sent to you, to beg that you will endeavor to ward off that plague."

O. M.—"Surely, I am ready and willing to do all that is in my power, to avert so disastrous a visitation as this disgraceful plague, which is worse in its effects than the black plague; the latter kills outright, but the former subjects its victims to a lifelong agony of disgrace and despair, from contemplation of the evil results of folly; but tell me, my daughter, what must I do, in order to shield you and your sisters from the 'Receiver's Plague'?"

C.—"Do this, my father: guarantee our bonds, so that we can fund our debts at a lower and more reasonable rate of interest; then we can settle with our creditors at from fifty to ninety cents on the dollar, and thereby relieve ourselves of about one-fourth of our debts. It would not be doing an injustice to our creditors, since those parties who at present hold our bonds, purchased them at from twenty-five to ninety cents on the dollar. The bondholders urge us to give them solid bonds, and offer, in case we agree, to compromise upon liberal terms. Hence, you see, that if you will guarantee our bonds, we can save about two per cent interest annually, and at the same time reduce our debt about one-fifth. To secure you, we will agree to limit our debts to—say about twenty per cent of our total assessed valuation. Such a course would establish business upon a firmer basis, and our increased prosperity would be to your advantage, since, as our business would increase, so would your Internal Revenue, which would enable you to liquidate your own indebtedness. The bondholders would say: 'I now have a bond that will be paid, both principal and interest, without its being necessary for me to employ an attorney to go into Court for the purpose of enforcing payment, and then perhaps fail. I now have a bond that I can use in bank as collateral security for about its face value, and I really believe that I could use it to pay hotel bills, even in Cairo, Egypt.' Now, you might say: 'Look here, Miss Delinquent, if you don't pay the interest and principal of these bonds, I will send my Marshal to oust you and collect the taxes until they are paid.' "

O. M.—"Well, Cincinnati, I am favorably impressed with your propositions, and I will present them to the next Congress for adoption; but tell me, how is it that you are so far behind in population, and yet so far advanced in debt? At one time, you were the Queen City of the West, but now St. Louis and Chicago are far ahead of you?"

C.—"My dear father, I attribute that to this: When the Jewish Hegira began from my Territory to Texas, I noticed a marked decline in the volume of trade, so, in order to offset that, I invested heavily in railroads; but when I had completed the system to the north, west, and southwest, I found it absolutely necessary to have a southern outlet, so I invested $18,000,000.00 in that road."

O. M.—"Oh! now I see where the trouble lies, you have been reading some work on railroads, and have got railroads on the brain."

C.—"Yes, I have been reading a book concerning the products of the country, and have built railroads in order to handle those products. Now, the book upon which I based all of my calculations, is one which I always considered to be perfectly reliable, from the fact that you appropriated money for its publication, and its title is "Helpers' Impending Crisis."

O. M.—"Oho! now I see why you were so anxious to have a southern outlet, it was to convey the hay, about which Helper wrote. Poor girl! I pity you, but I will try and help you out."

THE CONVENTION OF THE THIRTY-EIGHT BROTHERS.

The Thirty-eight Brothers, having arrived at man's estate, being of sound mind, and capable of managing their own affairs, without either the interference of each other or the "old man," met at Philadelphia in 1876, and having discussed the results of the late war, mutually agreed to let by-gones be by-gones, and to devote themselves to the re-establishment of confidence among the business community of the country. It was considered prudent and safe, both for the debtor and creditor, to establish one head bureau at Washington; the said bureau to have all powers, vested by act of Congress, in the Home Bond Bill.

As the United States Government was found to be in debt, beyond her ability to pay, without the assistance of the brothers, which comes in the shape of Internal Revenue, they (the brothers) demanded that the Government guarantee their bonds, and act as the head of the Bureau. Such being the sense of the convention, Maryland, being nearest to the seat of Government, was delegated to proceed to the White House, and present the petitions to the "old man."

MARYLAND'S INTERVIEW WITH THE "OLD MAN."

Maryland, arriving at the White House, enters without any ceremony, and says: "Good day, Dad!"

Old Man.—"How is this, Maryland, that you rush in as unceremoniously as if you had an important message from a national bank committee. But I know your failing, and I had a good deal of trouble with you during the late war, keeping you down. You are the boy who urged Virginia to raise the Confederate flag, on Arlington Heights, in sight of the White House. I have made a soldiers' cemetery of the Heights—"

Maryland.—"Yes, and over the gates of that cemetery you should cause to be written: 'Here rest the remains of Federal soldiers, who sacrificed their lives in battle to sustain, perpetuate, and give power to the Union; a power that is now being used to oppress her children by the imposition of heavy taxes for the benefit of the national banks and other chartered right's gentry, who never shouldered a musket in defense of that Union.'"

O. M.—"My son, do not forget yourself, remember to whom you are talking, if you have any business to transact with me, state it briefly, for I am in no very good humor to-pay."

M.—"Well, father, I am sorry to find you in a bad humor, for the business I have to transact with you is of such a nature that both parties should be in good humor. Nevertheless, I am here in behalf of my brothers, who petition you to guarantee our bonds. They are similar to those mentioned by sister Cincinnati and young Jackson, with this exception, that some of our bonds are to be of small denomination, say twenty-fives and fifty dollar bonds, in order that poor people can invest their savings, and not suffer loss, as has been the case heretofore, through the so-called savings banks."

O. M.—"If you boys continue to conduct your State affairs as heretofore, I decline to guarantee your bonds. I have noticed that where some of your treasurers defaulted, your courts failed to convict them ; so unless you show some disposition to be more vigilant, I will not guarantee the bonds. You boys received your share of the estate in 1776, and you have no claims upon me, so good-bye, Maryland."

M.—O no, father, not good-bye yet ! I must defend myself and my brothers, against your accusations. I denounce your usurpation of power which we did not confer upon you, and in my turn, I must beg that you will not forget yourself, but that you remember to whom you are talking. Who are you, I say, but the creature of our creation. We thirteen brothers, inherited all of this great domain from our mother's side, and you have nothing except that which we gave you, and that was life, name, and limited power. The constitution sets forth your duties, but of late years, you have ignored that instrument, which you swore to obey and defend, as though, like a monarch, you were not amenable to criminal law. You are drifting along the channel of pride, usurpation, and corruption, and if you do not look back and remember where you originated, you may land upon a tyranical foundation, similar to that occupied to-day, by that Grand Brute William, of the so-called German Empire. He claims to rule by divine right, he is supported by Bismarck, the Grand Intriguer, who says to the people, away with religion,

I will have none of it; if the people must have something to worship, let them worship the King. So do not forget yourself; you rule by the will of thirty-eight brothers. We created you and can annihilate you; and by a three-fourths vote, we can either add to, or take away your power. Do not take offense at my comparing you with William and Bismarck, that is done for the sake of illustration. You two are the only governments that, for the past twenty years, have been infringing upon the rights of the people; not by delegated right, but by force of arms and usurpation. You have taken from us things that, under the original contract, did not belong to you. We do not claim the right of secession, but we do claim the right of protection; that is, if any brother should violate his obligations to the constitution, to the injury of the other brothers, then it is your duty to compel him to live up to his contract; so if you overstep your delegated power, we brothers, have a right to compel you to live up to *your* contract. Do not deceive yourself, and imagine that the people owe allegiance to you individually; they only owe allegiance to you collectively. This Government is a sort of joint-stock company, and every citizen is a stockholder. Do not deceive yourself, and do as the devil did to Christ, and say, "Profess allegiance to me, and I will give you all these lands." It appears that you have been tempting the Pacific railroads by giving them lands which did not belong to you. Those lands are ours, we inherited them from our mother, and merely put you in charge of them. You should dispose of these lands for the benefit of all, and not for the benefit of the few. Do not forget that God created man for the public good, and the Devil being of an envious disposition, created Judas, Bismarck & Company for public bad; and as Judas, Stanton, Holt & Company ended, so may you, William, Bismarck, and the others end, who have no regard for an oath. Profit by the example of others, confine yourself to your prescribed duties only, so that when you go out of office, you may bear with you the respect of all people, instead of doing as Buchanan did, going to some obscure town, there to pine away, from the contemplation of the evil results of your official acts. Who was your forefather? You had none! We thirteen brothers created you, named you "Uncle Sam," and provided you with support and a homestead. As we were scattered all over the country, it was necessary for us to have some one who could transact business for us collectively, and to act as guardian for the minor boys, until they became of age. Individually, how have you discharged the duties of your office? I say, badly; for, by your extravagance, you have gone into debt, beyond your ability to pay, without calling upon us through a scheme called the Internal Revenue. You tell us that we have managed badly; that we have contracted enormous debts for which we have but little or nothing to show. But in your own case, take the cost of your Navy from 1860 to date, and what have you to show for that? A third rate Navy, not sufficiently strong to compel a third-rate power like Spain to make redress for her wholesale massacre of Americans, an outrage for which there was no manner of excuse. True the victims of the "Virginius massacre," may have forfeited their rights to citizenship, and hence to protection, by their joining the cruise, but there were many of the crew, who were entirely ignorant of the true character and mission of the vessel. You merely demanded the trial of Captain Buriel; he was tried and dismissed, and you were satisfied. Six months afterward he was promoted. How did you act in regard to extending protection to our citizens in Central America? When Walker's men offered to surrender, it was upon condition that they be permitted to return home. The terms were accepted, but after the men had lain down their arms, they were ordered to be shot. A petition was addressed to the American Consul begging him to save their lives; but he either *would* not or *could* not do it. They then invoked the aid of the British Consul, and *he* saved their lives. The men returned to New Orleans in worse trim than when they embarked, but with their stock of knowledge augmented; they had learned by bitter experience to place no confidence in either United States Consuls or passports. What does Bismarck care for an American passport? When he needs recruits for his armies, and catches Germans visiting their Fatherland, he makes soldiers of them. They apply to the American Minister and consulate for protection, and an investigation is had—with what result? Champagne and Bismarck diplomacy are brought to bear and the matter is dropped, but the visitors serve until the war is over. How have you managed your Indian affairs? You have been chasing the Indians over the plains of Dakota with disastrous results, and at a cost of millions of dollars. You have attempted their civilization, *i. e.* their subjugation. Finally you send private citizens, DeSmet, Gilpin, and others, to try and persuade the Indians to come into a reservation, and the Indian says to himself, "As we have been chased all summer, and had no time to lay in a stock of meat for the winter, we will go in and fatten up for next summer." This expensive Indian hunting should be put a stop to, and the money hitherto expended in that amusement, should be lent to private parties to build railroads through the Indian country, wherever railroads have appeared, the Indian has disappeared. If railroads are built through those sections where the Indian finds his winter quarters, he will have but one, of two alternatives, to leave, or to submit to government terms; but do not lend money on second mortgage, as was the case with the Pacific railroads, and do not locate the Indians on the sterile wastes of Dakota, but give them fertile lands two hundred acres to each member of a family, with the proviso that no Indian shall sell his land until he shall have occupied it fifty years. An army officer and a sufficient number of men should be placed or stationed on the reservation for police duty. The Government should provide the Indians with necessary farming implements, and encourage them in the cultivation of the soil. And in order to facilitate the induction of the Indian to the art of farming, the Government should donate farms of two hundred acres to those white or colored families who will settle in the reservation and teach the Indians the art of agriculture. The proportion of white or colored families to Indian families should be as one is to ten. The Government to supply the white, colored, and Indian families with provisions during a period of twenty years, commencing with a full supply the first year, and reducing it one-twentieth each succeeding year, for by that time it is presumable that they will have learned to support themselves. At the expiration of forty years, the Indians to come under the general law, to pay taxes as do other people. Those who are able to read and write to be allowed a vote, and as soon as the Government deems it safe, the troops to be withdrawn. The Government to erect school houses upon the reservation and maintain a corps of teachers for twenty years from its establishment. The Government not to attempt to Christianize the Indian, as that is no part of its duty. Let the missionaries of the various religious denominations settle among themselves as to which shall have the honor of converting them to Christianity. I will illustrate the manner in which the Government Christianized the Indians on the Missouri River agencies, at the Grand River agency there were over three thousand Indians and the first lesson in Christianity is taught by the officers, who win from the " Bucks " their best looking girls. In proof of which fact, I cite the number of half-breed children that are running about the reservation. Such acts exasperate the " Bucks," and they swear vengeance against the "pale face." The next lesson is received from the sutler, who teaches them the Christian art of cheating, another is received from the soldiery, who introduce syphilitic diseases, so that in the end, the fate of the Indian is worse than at the beginning, but this picture is true of Indians on frontier reservations. I advocate locating them in small colonies, near populous districts, where they can be subjected to the refining influence of a higher civilization and Christianity. From contact with such people, they would learn of the Three Fundamental Pillars that support the Nine Fundamental Principles of Christianity and civilization, the Jew, the

Mason, and the Catholic. From the Jew they will acquire a knowledge of God's Law, and commerce, and trade. From the Mason, they will learn that from the white light of knowledge springs peace and good will towards all men; that a man is a man and only a man. From the Catholic they will learn industry, obedience, and virtue. As the three Rulers in Heaven are the Father, Son, and Holy Ghost; the three rulers upon earth are Jew, Mason, and Catholic, and the three rulers in hell are the Devil, Pride, and Envy. Go where you will, there will you find the Jew among the speculators, the Mason among the rulers, and the Jesuit among the people, the latter always on hand when wanted and often when not wanted, to preach the doctrine of Rome. The Jew has a hard part to perform, since it was ordained that he shall have no permanent place of abode, but shall be a wanderer upon the face of the earth. He, the Jew, is one of God's miracles, left here to prove the truth of Holy Writ, the existence of God, and the Crucifixion of Christ his Son. Without the Jew, ministers of the gospel would have no visible proof of Christ ever having been upon earth.

You have endeavored to establish, by legal enactment, "Social Equality," when you know there can be no such thing, either in heaven, the earth, hell, or the penitentiary. Is it to be supposed that in case his Satanic Majesty falls heir to such giant intellects as Beecher, Bismarck, Ingersoll, and other cattle of a kindred ilk, that he will make of them common stokers? No, sir; they will be furnished with letters of marque and reprisal, and sent back from whence they came, to continue their fallacious reasoning, to divert the minds of people from the contemplation of the one true God, and to swell the cohorts of hell — a place that Beecher says does not exist. Of late years you have been interfering in our elections, for which course you have no right, without amending the Constitution. Read over that solemn writing, which at your inaugural you swore to uphold and protect; and if therein you can find any authority for appointing supervisors of elections, then it is a new construction of the real meaning

,ing of the Constitution, and different from that taught us by
our forefathers. We object to your supervisors, as it is
possible for them to be even more corrupt than the super-
vised ; in proof of which fact I refer you to your supervisors
under the ambitious regime of the Third Termers; they
compelled the distillers to be corrupt, or close their distill-
eries, therefore we want none of your supervisors. If we
should acknowledge your right to appoint supervisors, then,
by precedent, you might assume the right to appoint judges
and clerks of elections, and finally, returning boards, and
if that came to pass, what guarantee would the people have
against corrupt or ambitious men, who might enter into
league with the railroad power. Having previously appointed
judges of the Supreme Court with that purpose in view, and
with the army sworn to obey the orders of the President,
and to support the decisions of the Courts, a corrupt and
ambitious man might cause himself to be counted in against
the will of the people. Hence, I claim, that by a central-
ization of the powers of the Government, the liberty of the
Republic is endangered ; but, by a division of those powers
among the States, we will have some guarantee for the per-
petuation of the Republic. I admit that there are some
laws, at present in the codes of the States, that should be
vested in the general government ; but it should be done in
a legal manner, in accordance with the Constitution, and not
by usurpation, as heretofore. You may think to enjoy the
pride of office, obtained through fraud, but remorse of con-
science will more than balance that enjoyment. You may
labor under the impression that there is no hereafter, if so, I
will recall to your mind some of the phantoms that have dis-
turbed your uneasy slumbers in the White House. Your
mind may have been wandering, thousands of miles away, in
fancied intrigue with Queen Vic. the miserly Popess of the
Church of England ; and, with Bismarck, to the end that they
recognize you as Emperor of North America ; but awake to the
truth, for it was given to man by the Great Father to dream.
While we brothers were fighting you took advantage of us and

took in Brother Nevada, before he was of age, in order to carry out your ill-advised schemes. You also adopted and took into the family of State, that illegitimate child, West Virginia, who, we refuse to acknowledge as a legitimate brother. You have neglected your duty in matters concerning home products, for Brother Louisiana tells me that you bought last year from foreign governments over $74,000,000 worth of sugar, while those same governments bought of us less than $7,000,000 of our products. Spain, who takes the largest amount of the said $74,000,000, places a prohibitory tariff of over $4.00 per barrel on our flour and other products in proportion. Louisiana tells me that he has swamp lands—enough, if they were drained, to raise sugar enough for the whole country, and thereby keep the $74,000,000 at home, and give employment to thousands of families. Louisiana is not able to drain those swamps, but you might buy and reclaim them. They could then be sold to settlers for more than enough to cover the expense of draining, to say nothing of improving the health of the people.

We propose to change the mode of electing you, for past experience has proven that the Electoral College system has been productive of trouble, controversy, and needless expense. It has been found wanting for the object had in view by our forefathers, and it has been the means of seating in the Presidential chair, seven minority Presidents. First—John Q. Adams, in 1824. Second—Jas. K. Polk, in 1844. Third—Z. Taylor, in 1848. Fourth—James Buchanan, in 1856. Fifth—A. Lincoln, in 1860. Sixth—R. B. Hayes, in 1876, and Seventh—James A. Garfield, in 1880, and it is but fair to presume that had not the troops interfered in the Southern States, during Grant's Presidential campaign, he would have been in the minority. When military officers can be used as they were used in South Carolina, in the interest of one party, against another, then the will of the people is easily defeated. When an officer of the U. S. Army will interest himself to such an extent, as not to ask for orders from his superior officer, but go himself to Washington City for orders from a partisan leader, and then place a sergeant at the door of a State capitol with orders to admit no member unless he have a certificate from a partisan judge appointed for that very purpose, then the *augur* in question is not a carpenter's tool, but a partisan tool. So from your past acts, and the possibility of usurpation and corruption in the future, we have decided to change your term of office to six years—limited to one term. We will grant you a pension of $10,000.00 per annum, to continue during the natural life of yourself and wife.˙ You are not to appoint to office any blood relation of either yourself or your wife, which will put a stop to such cases as Fred Grant's. You are to be elected by the popular vote, each political party to have an equal number of representatives at all places of registration, if any, at all polling places, and upon all returning boards. One bad precedent can do more harm than four good ones can amend. An evil-disposed President will conduct himself well during his first term in order to gain the confidence of the people, so that he can perfect his corrupt schemes during his second term. Take Napoleon, the Cæsars, Grant, and others, it was the people to begin with, but the great *I am* to end with."

I now close, and submit my schemes, my propositions, and my bills to my reader. Whether they are worthy of approval must be left to his judgment. I feel that I have performed my duty in endeavoring to prove that in the administration of public affairs, every American citizen is entitled to a vote, and an opinion. I am aware that my ideas are crude and are presented in an unfinished manner, but I trust that men of greater knowledge and literary attainments than myself, will find enough herein to warrant them in taking up the matter, and presenting it in the shape that I feel it deserves.

I do not claim perfection for my work, but I consider it to be the foundation and basis of measures, which, when reduced to practical working, will redound to the benefit of the people of this great Republic.

Very Respectfully,

MAT. KONCEN.

St. Louis, Mo., April 10, 1881.

ANNEX.

As has been shown by the adoption of the $30 and $32 per capita schemes, $285,000,000 legal tenders will have to be issued, all of which will have been redeemed in coin within twenty years, by means of the other schemes, and there will yet remain an annual surplus of over one million dollars from the appropriated revenue. A further annual surplus will result from the $300,000,000 at present allowed as the annual expense of the Government, from the fact that the river improvement scheme, as herein proposed, will do away with the necessity of an appropriation on that account; so that altogether an unappropriated surplus of about five million dollars may be estimated. That sum should be applied as follows: First in the construction of five or more steamships specially designed for privateering, and combining speed and strength, capable of being quickly handled in close quarters. These vessels should be supplied with such armaments as the Navy Department may deem proper. Two of the vessels should be stationed on the Pacific and three on the Atlantic coast. The United States Government should never relinquish her right of privateering since it is her best safeguard in the event of European wars. Five good privateers can do more to avert, or bring to a close, a war with a government like England, than half a million soldiers, or the English Channel full of unwieldy gun-boats.

In times of peace the said vessels could be placed in commission as United States mail and passenger packets to run between our Atlantic and Pacific ports, and South American, Indian, or other commercial ports, which at present need a greater tonnage to accommodate the demands of commerce. The placing of these vessels as mail and passenger packets between those ports would, in a few years, result in more intimate commercial relationship, and would induce private parties to establish lines of steamers; it would ultimately result in a revival of American commerce at a much less expense than that attending the granting of subsidies to private monopolies. Again, by placing these vessels in commission as mail and passenger packets, we can build up the American marine, since the youth would prefer enlisting upon such a class of vessels to enrolling themselves in such training ships as the Wachussets, where the boys never knew whether the vessel would ever leave port or not, or in case she did leave, never knew her destination or how long she would be out. But if my plan is adopted, the boys will say to each other, " let's go, for we will see the whole world in a short time, and if we don't like the ship, we can soon leave as she often comes into port." After building the said privateers, and paying for them, the said surplus of five million to be used in the redemption of legal tenders.

REDUCTION OF TAXES.

Taking the year 1880 as a basis, the receipts from all sources amounted to $361,000,000, which amount, according to the hereinbefore mentioned schemes, is all assigned to particular purposes. If the Government suffers no reverses it is fair to anticipate an annual increase in revenue on account of the annual increase in population and business. Such being the case, the revenue resulting from " internal revenue," or imports should not be permitted to exceed $361,000,000, at which amount the receipts should be held. An annual surplus will remain from the receipts as there will be an annual reduction in disbursements. In 1880 $73,652,000 was paid on account of the public debt, $95,757,000 on interest, $56,700,000 on pensions, and $2,795,000 on premium on bonds. Two of said items, viz: The interest on the public debt and pensions will show an annual reduction, and thus would result an annual surplus for Congressmen to skirmish with, to further reduce taxes, or to redeem legal tenders with coin as might be deemed best.

THE AMERICAN CANCER.

There is a silent and constant drain upon the resources of the American people, with which to meet the interest upon our securities held abroad, such as United States bonds, State and city bonds, railroad bonds, mining stocks, lands, etc. It is a well-known fact that foreigners hold the first mortgage bonds of the railways, which, on account of rascally management upon the part of some railroad presidents, in that they have borrowed money upon the bonds to pay dividends, must come to an end, the railways must be sold under those mortgages, so that the foreigner will receive just double the amount of what he now holds, and the stockholder will lose everything. The London *Economist*, of 1878, says that American securities held abroad amount to over $3,500,- 000,000, which at 6 per cent would yield $210,000,000. So according to that journal the people of the United States pay annually to foreigners interest on various securities amounting to $210,000,000. The duties on imports show the balance of trade to be in our favor, but it has to show $210,000,000 annually before the interest on those securities is balanced, and hence I am justified in alluding to that drain as the American cancer.

APPENDIX.

APPENDIX

APPENDIX "A."

Financial condition of the United States Government, January 1, 1881, as per Secretary Sherman's Public Debt Statement, January 3, 1881:

Total coin bonds	$1,672,665,400	00
Non-interest bearing debt, viz:		
Legal tenders, fractional currency, certificates of deposit, and coin certificates	427,619,696	00
Total debt	$2,100,285,096	00
Cash in Treasury	$222,299,739	
Amount due by Pacific Railroads, principal and interest	79,994,592	
Total deduction	302,294,331	00
Balance, net debt	$1,797,990,765	00
Debt per capita, based upon population of 1880	35	83
Receipts from Internal Revenue, Customs, and other sources, 1880	359,496,739	00
Appropriation for 1881	298,055,097	00
Surplus	$61,441,642	00

Comptroller's currency report, January 1, 1881:

Legal Tenders	$346,681,016	00
National Bank Notes	343,219,943	00
Demand notes, compound interest notes, and fractional currency	19,368,481	00
Coin in circulation	612,283,357	00
Total circulation	$1,321,552,797	00
Per capita circulation January 1, 1881	26	55

(St. Louis Financial Chronicle, January 10, 1881.)

Money in the hands of the people...................... $843,107,462 00
Per capita in the hands of the people................. 16 81

NOTE—Sherman, in his report, says that there may be deducted from the total debt, $12,000,000, fractional currency lost, and $1,000,000 paper money destroyed in the Chicago fire.

APPENDIX "B."

Secretary's report to Congress, under date of January 10th, 1880 showing expenses from 1861 to 1879, including the expenses of the war:

Interest on the public debt........................... $1,764,256,198 00
Pay of two and three year volunteers................. 1,040,102,702 00
Subsistence of the army. 381,417,548 00
Clothing of the army................................. 345,543,880 00
Transportation....................................... 336,793,885 00
Horses 126,672,423 00
Other Quartermaster supplies......................... 320,000,000 00
Pensions... 407,429,193 00
Bounties... 140,281,178 00
Reimbursing the State for war expenses............... 41,000,000 00
Arms... 76,000,000 00
Supplies... 56,000,000 00
Assessing and collecting revenue..................... 113,000,000 00
Expenses for National loan and currency.............. 51,523,000 00
Premium on gold...................................... 59,738,000 00
Expenses of the Navy................................. 412,000,000 00
National cemeteries.................................. 5,243,000 00
Support of "National Home" for disabled volunteers. 8,546,000 00

Total war expenses......... .... $5,685,547,007 00
Ordinary expenses of Government during the nineteen
   years.. 609,549,143 00

Grand total for the nineteen years.............. $6,295,096,150 00

NOTE—Cost of the war per capita based on the census of 1880, $113 36-100.

APPENDIX "C."

Oakland and Barges—Crying Evil.

WASHINGTON, June 10.—When the river and harbor bill was consid-ered in the Senate an amendment was adopted directing that a survey be made with a view of ascertaining the practicability and cost of construction of a ship canal from Lake Erie, by the Maumee and Wabash valleys, in the bed of the old Wabash and Erie canal, to the navigable waters of the Wabash river; also for a survey and estimate of cost of a similar canal from Junction City, on the Wabash and Erie canal, to the Ohio river, by way of the Miami and Erie canal, to produce the most practical and least expensive ship canal from Lake Erie to the navigable waters of the Ohio river, the estimates to be for a water channel and locks of the same size and capacity as those of the enlarged Erie canal in New York.

While the Senate was doing this the House Committee on Railways and Canals had adopted a bill covering the same ground and appropriating $15,000 for expenses. A very interesting report has been prepared by Mr. Wise, and as it treats of a matter in which the West is materially interested, I give the essential features. It is well known that the rapid progress of improvements at the Welland canal makes it an important matter to secure water-communication between the western rivers and the lakes.

"It will be observed," says the committee, "that our internal water-routes by nature are divided up into subdivisions or systems, of which the great Mississippi River system, including all its branches, is the greatest in extent and importance. Secondly, the great lake system is next in extent and importance. Then we have the Hudson River, the Connecticut River, the James River, and many others.

"Now, if we connect any two of these rivers by an artificial channel, so as practically to convert the two into one, we not only make the one combination of more than double the extent, but of vastly more than double in amount of traffic and commercial importance.

"If, now, we put in another link in the form of a large canal, first-class in all its appointments, connecting the Mississippi system with the lakes, can any one doubt that the Upper Mississippi and its tributaries will pour a vast commerce into the lakes, and thence into the Hudson, and that these latter will in turn abundantly contribute of their greatly increased accumulations to the Mississippi? The importance, the necessity of a water connection between our lake ports and our interior and marine ports for the use and sustenance of the navy in unforeseen events that are liable to arise at any unexpected time must be so evident to all that we deem it unnecessary to more than call attention to this subject, and to the further fact that should such events arise it will then be too late to commence a work that requires years for its execution.

"Your committee further desires to call attention to the important fact that while we as a nation have continually neglected (except the limited aid contributed to the Erie canal alone) to furnish any aid or means to cheapen transportation and enlarge the outlets from the great lakes east through our own domain and through our own cities and ports, our British cousins have been constantly and wisely enlarging and vastly improving their outlet from the upper lakes through the Welland canal and the St. Lawrence. They are successfully competing with us in carrying our own grain and other produce from our own lake cities to Europe, and shortly they will have their water routes so enlarged and improved that foreign vessels of two thousand tons capacity, coming by a route owned and controlled by a foreign power, can enter all our upper lake cities, while the limit of capacity of boats passing by our Erie canal is but six hundred and ninety tons each.

"Further, as to the practicability of either of these routes, there can be no doubt, as canals have long since been constructed, and are still in practical use upon them, and are peculiarly favored with abundant water supplies upon their summit levels, one of which—the Miami and Erie—has the largest artificial lake or reservoir in the world, and which, with but little additional expense, can be made to feed abundantly the enlarged ship canal proposed.

"It is evident that the low freights on water routes, and their controlling effect in keeping down railroad freights nearly as low as their own, alone enables Western farmers and dealers to ship corn, oats, and other cheap grains to Europe, which they only can do profitably during the season of water-route competition.

"We report in favor of ʟ complete examination of the two routes which converge into one at Junction City, Ohio, and form one route from that place to Toledo, with no natural opposition of any consequence to overcome, but at every point favorable and inviting."—*Correspondence of the Republican.*

———————

. St. Paul, December 20.—The St. Paul Board of Trade to-day adopted the following:

Resolved, That the people of Minnesota are losing millions of dollars every year in the extra freight they are compelled to pay for the transportation of their products to the markets of the world, and upon all articles of necessity imported to the State, and since the only hope of relief from these evils is in the opening up of competing water lines of transportation, we call upon our Representatives in Congress to insist upon the improvement of the Mississippi River and lakes, and to stand together as one man, with all Representatives of the Northwest, in opposition to all sections and all interests which oppose these improvements.

Resolved further, That a copy of this resolution be forwarded to each of our Representatives in Congress with the request that they confer with Representatives of Wisconsin, Iowa, and other sections interested in these improvements, with a view to unity of action and the formation of a league, offensive and defensive, for the success of these measures.

THIS was sought to be shown in Friday's issue of the *Republican*, and the statement was reliable as based on the statistics supplied by the Secretary of the Merchants' Exchange in his report of the trade and commerce of the city for 1880. The object of the summary given in the *Republican* was to show what had been done and was doing for our grain business in the facilities, extent, and prospects of movement by the river to foreign countries, and in it were contained all the data to the present, so far as practical capacity was concerned. As further evidence of what can be done here in immense movement of grain by river southward for export—and all in bulk that goes by that route is for export—is given the cargo of wheat and corn by a single fleet which left this port yesterday, that of the steamer Oakland, of the St. Louis and New Orleans Transportation line, which will take into New Orleans (dangers of navigation excepted) the largest tow of grain that ever descended the Mississippi, including 263,465 bushels of corn, and 90,000 bushels wheat, or a total of 10,465 tons, or 20,847,900 pounds. This great quantity has been received by eight barges, six of which left yesterday morning, the remaining two to be added at Belmont, to which point a portion of the grain had been transported from here by the St. Louis, Iron Mountain and Southern Railroad. In addition to this immense towage by the Oakland will be taken a capacious fuel barge, and the whole, it is known, she can handle with ease. The largest previous tows in 1880 were as follows in the order of proportions of bushels and pounds: The Iron Mountain and barges left the levee April 10, with 300,000 bushels of corn, or 16,800,000 pounds cargo. The same boat and barges, February 29. with 47,000 bushels wheat, and 210,228 bushels corn, or 14,392,768 pounds. The D. Gilmore, July 17, with 178,000 bushels wheat, and 30,000 bushels corn, or 13,860,000 pounds; and the Oakland, August 10, with 230,158 bushels wheat. And these figures comprise mainly wheat and corn, rye playing a comparatively small part, yet promising well as a factor in the interest of grain export from here. There were other large movements of grain by the barge lines last year, but they need not now be mentioned. It is worthy of note in connection with the above, that this single cargo of the Oakland would have required 700 freight cars to have carried the same amount on thirty-five separate freight trains and engines.

APPENDIX "D."

Conkling and Railroads vs. United States Courts—Railroad Influence in United States Courts.

Restrained From Paying Taxes.

SAN FRANCISCO, Feb. 21.—A bill in equity was filed to-day in the United States Circuit Court by C. P. Huntington to restrain the Central and Southern Pacific Railroads and their branches from paying, and the tax collectors of the different counties through which they pass from collecting, the taxes levied on the basis of the assessment fixed by the State Board of Equalization. Fifty suits have been drawn covering every mile of railroad owned by the two companies in this State. Complaint alleges that the tax and assessment are void on constitutional grounds. First, because the bill under which the assessment was made embraced more than one subject; second, because the clause of the constitution dividing the executive, legislative, and judicial powers of the government is infringed by the act of the board of equalization; third, because the board did not assess the property at its actual value; fourth, the board did not assess the improvements separately as the law provides. Judge Sawyer granted a restraining order summoning the defendants to show cause why an injunction should not be granted returnable next Monday.—*Missouri Republican Feb. 22, 1881.*

A Question of Water.

The application of the elevated railroads of New York for relief from the $750,000 taxes assessed against them for the last two years has been refused, and if the statements of the officers made in the presentation of their case be true, the companies must go into bankruptcy. But the New York public do not believe these statements. It may be true that the roads can not, after paying their operating expenses, taxes and interest, pay also a dividend on their $48,000,000 stock; but it is asserted that this stock consists of a large amount of water—some estimates make it seven-eighths and others four to one. Two of the roads show an aggregate of stock, bonds and other securities issued of $24,641,000; but a legislative commission estimated that their to actual cost has been only $18,358,000. For the first two years after the roads went into operation reports were circulated of their large business and large profits, under which the stock advanced strongly in price. After this came stories of suits, extraordinary legal proceedings and insecurity of structures, which caused a fall in prices. The fluctuations were from 20 to 50 per cent and it is asserted that the managers of the roads profited largely by availing themselves of these reports started by themselves; and the suspicion is expressed that the present complaint about the insufficiency of the earnings to pay the demands upon them are part of a new game of stock-jobbing. The admitted gross earnings of the roads last year were $5,200,000, and these are steadily increasing; and the public take the view that the net earnings are sufficient to pay a dividend on the actual cost of the roads, if the owners would only be content with that.—*Missouri Republican.*

Railroad Influence in Court.

A telegram was yesterday sent to Senator Thurman, as Chairman of the Judiciary Committee of the Senate, signed by the President and Secretary of the New York Board of Trade and Transportation, "in behalf of 800 business firms," members of that organization, protesting against the confirmation of Stanley Matthews as Associate Justice of the Supreme Court of the United States on these grounds:

1. That the railroad corporations are endeavoring to obtain control of that Court, which has heretofore been the most important bulwark in defending the public interests against the encroachments of corporations.

2. That Mr. Matthews has been educated as a railroad lawyer and naturally regards railroad questions from that point now.

3. That Mr. Matthews' action in the Senate proves this and shows that in this important respect he is unfit for the position for which he has been nominated by the President.

This telegram is deserving of and will receive careful consideration from the Judiciary Committee of the Senate, whose able Chairman is thoroughly familiar with the matters mentioned therein. The telegram shows clearly that the merchants are keeping their eyes wide open for the movements of the railroad monopolists and will not be slow in using means to thwart their machinations against the interests of the people.— *New York Graphic.*

Exempt from Taxation.

WHEELING, W. Va., May 2.—In the case of the Chesapeake and Ohio Railway Co. against J. S. Miller, auditor of West Virginia, Judge Mel-

via to-day delivered an opinion refusing to dissolve the injunction heretofore granted restraining the assessment and collection of taxes on the
property of the road. The effect of this decision is to sustain the position of the company that its property is exempt from taxation under the
original act of incorporation.

The New York correspondent of the Detroit *Free Press* says:

THE most eloquent and, at the same time, most authoritative tribute to
the power of money, in its organized and working shape, may be found
in the following extract from the report of the United States Senate
Committee on Transportation Routes:

"In the matter of taxation, there are to-day four men representing
the four great trunk lines between Chicago and New York, who possess,
and who not infrequently exercise, powers which the Congress of the
United States would not venture to exert. They may at any time, and
for any reason satisfactory to themselves, by a single stroke of the pen,
reduce the value of property in this country by hundreds of millions of
dollars. An additional charge of five cents per bushel on the transportation of cereals would have been equivalent to a tax of forty-five millions of dollars on the crop of 1873. No Congress would dare to exercise so vast a power except upon a necessity of the most imperative
nature; and yet these gentlemen exercise it whenever it suits their
supreme will and pleasure, without explanation or apology."

Occasionally it assumes to dictate in quarters where dictation has
hitherto been considered impossible. For instance, last January, in an
argument before the Supreme Court of the United States, Mr. Franklin
B. Gowen said:

"I have heard the counsel of the Pennsylvania Railway Company,
standing in the Supreme Court of Pennsylvania, threaten that court with
the displeasure of its clients if it decided against them, and all the blood
in my body tingled with shame at the humiliating spectacle."

Mr. Gowen's rather significant statement has never been contradicted.

Of course the money power buys fine tools when it needs them. For
instance, during the war the federal government, under the then existing tax laws, collected $500,000 from the New York Central Railway
Company. Sometime afterward the company—which had always dis-
puted the legality of the tax—brought suit against the government for
the amount, and hired Senator Conkling as its attorney. He gained his
case; by what arguments the Utica *Observer* gently indicates:

"Now, when Mr. Conkling went down to Canandaigua to try this
railroad case, he carried with him a greater political influence than any
other man in our State wields. He appeared before a judge whom he
had elevated to the bench only a few months before. He confronted a
district attorney who could not hold his office for a day if Mr. Conkling
should demand his removal. He secured a verdict which the jury was

forced to render by the rulings of the judge. Under that verdict the railroad recovers a round half million, which it might have lost but for its shrewdness in employing the right man to prosecute its claim."

And the New York *Tribune* said:

"The appearance of Senator Conkling as attorney in a recent railroad case, in behalf of a railroad corporation and against the government of which he is a sworn official, suggests a question of political expediency, and incidentally of morals, which must sooner or later be very fully and freely discussed before the people. * * * Somewhere there must be a line which separates the profession of an advocate from the functions of a legislator. Would it not be well to have that line authoritatively defined?"

To all of which Senator Conkling and his employers may reply, " Well, what are you going to do about it?"—and nobody can answer the interesting question.

Evidently we have in our midst a moneyed aristocracy more influential for good or evil than all the blue-blooded nobility of the Old World; more powerful even than the agents of the people in Congress assembled. And again the interesting question arises, " What are we going to do about it?"—*Clipped from the Missouri Republican, Dec, 12, 1880.*

APPENDIX "E."

Pacific R. R. Government—R. R. Candidates—Rivers and Railroads.

A Railroad Candidate.

It would be very interesting to have the full strength of the railroads put forward in such a struggle, because then we should have an opportunity of learning, under the most favorable circumstances, what the railroad strength amounts to. Heretofore, in the contests between the railroad corporations and the popular governing bodies, we have seen only isolated and individual exertions of strength, although it is to be noted that in every case the railroads have come out ahead. Thirteen years ago the Missouri Railroads tackled the Missouri Legislature, and when the conflict was over, the railroad people had all the property and the people of the State had all the load to carry. Three years ago the Hannibal and St. Joe Railroad, single-handed and unaided, bucked against the State, and the State fared no better than a country bumpkin in a bunko den. We do not need to recall the success with which the Pacific Railroad corporations first extracted from the

Treasury enough money to build the roads and then beat the National Government on a plain question of paying interest on the debt which created the railroads. There has never been a conflict between a railroad corporation and a department of government, State, National or municipal, in which the railroad did not come out ahead, and this even in cases where the railroads were comparatively weak and wholly unaided.—*St. Louis Globe-Democrat.*

Pacific Railroads.

SINKING FUNDS.

WASHINGTON, Feb. 15.—The Secretary of the Interior transmitted to the House to-day an important communication from the Auditor of Railroad Accounts.

The condition of the debt of these companies to the United States may be stated as follows: Union Pacific, principal, $27,236,512; interest to December 31, 1879, $19,238,182; total, $46,474,694; repaid by transportation and cash, $9,826,638; balance December 31, 1879, $36,648,056; add two years' interest, 1880 and 1881, $3,268,381; total, $39,916,437; less payments under the Thurman law of 1880–81, $3,750,000; balance Dec. 31, 1881, $36,166,437.

Central Pacific—Principal $27,855,680; interest to Dec. 31, 1879, $19,271,111; total, $47,126,791; repaid by transportation or cash, $4,541,318; balance Dec. 31, 1879, $42,585,437; add two years' interest—1880 and 1881—$3,342,682; total, $46,928,155; less payments under the Thurman law—1880 and 1881—$2,100,000; balance Dec. 31, 1881, $43,828,155.

THE New York Central Railroad represents $130,000,000 of investment, and $30,000,000 of annual business. The Pennsylvania Road represents $150,000,000, and $40,000,000 of business; the Union and Central Pacific represent between them nearly $300,000,000. A mortgage was filed last week in St. Louis, on a single railroad, for $50,000,000. Enormous as are these figures, they are but the beginning, or rather the first landing-place, in a course of consolidation which is part of the destiny of railroads. Our country is very large, and the necessities of competition compel the owners of railroad property to unite vast systems under one management. The greater the mileage of our railroads, the greater the investment, the business and the influence, the smaller the number of corporations, and in a very few years we will find the whole railroad property of this country under the management and control of a dozen or so of magnates, united in purpose, inexhaustible in resources and not over-scrupulous in the use of them. Any one who stops to think of it, can not help thinking that the country is in less danger from any third-term movement than it is from the influence of railroad corporations. As the test has got to come, and as the sooner it comes the better.

APPENDIX "G."

Decrease of Timber.

THE Vice-President of the Western Lumbermen's Exchange estimates that, if the demand for lumber increases proportionately, the forests of the United States will be annihilated in twenty years. The same view is taken by the *Northwestern Lumberman*, which says that "the timber supply of the Northwest is becoming so rapidly exhausted that within the next ten years something like a timber famine may be looked for."

APPENDIX "H."

Local Departments.

Rivers and Railroads.

Eastern members of Congress object to the appropriation of $1,000,000 for the improvement of the Mississippi river below Cairo because they fear that it would commit the Government to an approval of the Mississippi River Commissioners' plan for the general improvement of that stream, and cost a great deal of money in the end. It is curious that these gentlemen should be so shocked at every imagined extravagance involved in appropriations to the great rivers of the West when we remember the readiness with which they voted for the enormous grants of lands to railroads owned by Eastern companies. A recent official statement gives some surprising facts about these land grants. The amount of public lands given to the Pacific railroads alone is 181,000,000 acres; of this the roads have sold $36,000,000 worth, at an average price of $4.25 per acre, and own 43,000,000 acres, valued at $78,889,000; and they have a claim on 61,907,000 acres more, valued at $134,000,000—the value of the whole grant being $248,000,000—and this exclusive of the $64,000,000 in bonds granted them in addition. It may be said that these roads are in the West. This is true, but they are owned by East- ern men, and in that fact we have the explanation of the lavish liberal- ity of Eastern members of Congress. These members were, many of them, stockholders in the companies, and, in voting for the land grants, they were simply voting large areas of the public domain to themselves.

It may be a geographical misfortune that the Mississippi river does not flow from west to east and empty into Long Island Sound or Massachusetts Bay, instead of the Gulf of Mexico. Were this the case, Eastern Representatives would find reasons for appropriating money for its improvement which they do not discern now. Still, the great river runs in its entire course through American territory, and as it washes ten States, one would think it as clearly entitled to a few millions of public money as are the railroads which have been voted land grants worth $248,000,000.—*Missouri Republican Feb. 12, 1881.*

Municipal Debts.

Gov. McClellan calls the attention of the New Jersey Legislature to the enormous load of indebtedness which some of the cities in that State are carrying. Nine of them have debts aggregating $36,500,000, or one-sixth of their total valuation of taxable property. Rahway owes at the rate of $243 for every man, woman and child within its limits. Gov. Hartranft also takes a gloomy view of the ability of Pennsylvania cities to meet their financial obligations, and many other States are not much better off in this respect than New Jersey and Pennsylvania.

States.	Local Indebtedness.
New York (census of 1875)...	$244,079,859
Pennsylvania ($78,000,000, according to the report of the Secretary of Internal Affairs, in 1878, to which must be added at least $50,000,000).........	128,000,000
New Jersey (special commission of 1879)......................................	47,314,802
Illinois (Assistant Auditor of the State)......................................	51,821,691
Ohio...	41,490,574
Massachusetts (Tax Commissioner's report)....................................	87,000,000
Wisconsin (Secretary of State), nearly....	10,000,000
Minnesota (statistical review), more than.....................................	5,500,000
Kansas (Auditor's report), more than...	13,000,000
Missouri (estimated in year-book of this year)	40,000,000
Connecticut (compiled in 1877)...	17,000,000
Rhode Island (State hand-book), about..	12,000,000
New Hampshire (Tax Commissioners), about.................................	5,500,000
California (Auditor's report), about..	11,000,000
Tennessee (Comptroller's report) nearly......................................	10,000,000
Iowa (Governor's message)...	6,000,000
Nevada (Comptroller's report)..	900,000
Indiana (State bureau of statistics), about....................................	14,000,000
Louisiana (Constitutional Convention)..	20,000,000
Total..	$764,206,926

To these totals may be added the totals in round numbers for the other States, as given in the United States census for 1870, which were as follows. Mr. Porter says that he does not expect to find very great changes in the amount of the local indebtedness of the States named below. The debt in most cases was small in these States in 1870, and there have been no causes since for a marked increase:

State.	Local Indebtedness.
Alabama	$ 4,800,000
Arkansas	700,000
Delaware	500,000
Florida	900,000
Georgia	15,000,000
Kentucky	15,000,000
Maine	8,500,000
Maryland	15,500,000
Michigan	4,000,000
Mississippi	700,000
Nebraska	1,500,000
North Carolina	2,500,000
Oregon	100,000
South Carolina	5,600,000
Texas	1,000,000
Vermont	2,500,000
Virginia	8,500,000
West Virginia	500,000
Total	$ 87,800,000
	764,206,926
Grand total	$852,006,926

APPENDIX "I."

Anti-Monopoly.

SENATE CHAMBER, WASHINGTON, Feb. 19.

The Hon. L. E. Chittenden, President National Anti-Monopoly League:

MY DEAR SIR.—I deeply regret that official duties of an imperative character prevent the acceptance of your kind invitation to address the meeting at Cooper Institute on the 21st inst. Until to-day I hoped to be able to arrange my business so as to attend the meeting, but find it will be impossible.

The purpose of your League, as I understand it, is not to wage war upon corporations or individuals, but conceding to all their just rights, to demand full protection for the rights of the citizen against the abuses and aggressions of corporate power, and to insist upon the enforcement of those principles of law and natural right defined by the Supreme Court of the United States. In this effort you have my most hearty sympathy and co-operation. Your cause is just, but in such a contest you grapple with giants. Do not underrate the power or the skill of your antagonists. Wise and conservative counsels will alone secure success. You must be as prompt to concede rights as you are determined in demanding them. No agrarian or communistic spirit must find a place in your proceedings. The character of the men who compose your organization give assurance against danger on this point. Constitutions, natural rights, and the spirit of our Institutions are on your side. Intrenched behind these and fighting for the right, you can not fail.

Corporate power has done much to develop our country. For its good deeds I freely accord it full credit. As an instrument to execute the will and serve the interests of the public, it is of incalculable value; but as the imperious ruler of the people it is a most cruel and relentless tyrant. Kept within the limits of proper restraint it is an invaluable servant of the public. Unrestrained by the forces of law and public opinion it will prove a most dangerous master. The individual citizen is impotent to contend with this gigantic and rapidly growing power. Governmental authority, State and National, alone is competent to restrain its aggressions and correct its abuses. I have long foreseen that the time would come when the people would be compelled to invoke the exercise of that authority for their protection. I repeat to-day, in substance, words uttered seven years ago, that "there are in this country four men who, in the matter of taxation, possess and frequently exercise powers which neither Congress nor any of our State Legislatures would dare to exert—powers which, if exercised in Great Britain would shake the throne to its very foundation. These men may at any time, and for any reason satisfactory to themselves, by a stroke of the pen, reduce the value of property in the United States by hundreds of millions. They may at their own will and pleasure disarrange and embarrass business, depress one city or locality and build up another, enrich one individual and ruin his competitors, and, when complaint is made, coolly reply, ' What are you going to do about it?' "

The men who wield this stupendous corporate power have grown wiser with the passage of events. Hitherto they have been apparently content to absorb and control the great industrial and material interests of the country by a monopoly of the channels and instruments of transportation, but recently new and alarming conditions are presented. They know full well that if the people can freely communicate with each other they will see the dangerous tendencies of this power and organize to restrain it. Hence, in order to lay deep and sure foundations for the maintenance of their power, and to defeat the efforts of the people to curb it, they have now seized upon the channels of thought. Look at it a moment. One man, who controls more miles of railroad than any other in the world, and who is almost daily adding new lines to his colossal combination, now also controls the telegraphic system of the United States and Canada, and is reaching under the sea to grasp that of Europe. Not content with all this, and determined that no instrument of commercial and political power shall elude his grasp, he is (as I learn) also the owner of three out of the seven newspapers which constitute the

Associated Press, through the agency of which the news is distributed over the entire country. He may at any time secure the fourth paper, which will give him absolute control over the news which the people shall receive. When that takes place what will be our condition? What choice will the people then have to resist the encroachments of corporate power? How shall they even communicate with each other on the subject? What opportunity will there be for a fair discussion of these questions? The daily news supplied to the myriad of newspapers must first pass under the supervision of one or two men, who represent the Associated Press, and who are appointed by its owner. They will have full authority, and doubtless will be required to suppress, add to, or color the information thus sent out as may best serve the interests, the ambition, or the malice of the man to whom they owe their places. Hence the 20,000,000 of people who read their morning papers at their breakfast tables will daily receive just such impressions as this one man shall choose to give them. Public men and affairs, and business interests and movements, will be seen in the coloring which shall best serve his interests. The legislator who shall then be bold enough to raise his voice in behalf of the people, or to strike a blow in their defense, will be misrepresented or denied a hearing before his own constituents. The business man who shall venture to question the divine right of corporate rule will be crushed, and no telegraphic wire or Associated Press will voice his woe or demand redress from his persecutors. The people will find themselves unable to communicate with each other except by the gracious will and pleasure of the autocrat of the wires. Should special correspondents undertake to supply information not deemed expedient to be sent by the Associated Press, they will find that the owner of the wires can supply a ready remedy for such presumption.

The channels of thought and the channels of commerce thus owned and controlled by one man, or by a few men, what is to restrain corporate power, or to fix a limit to its exactions upon the people? What is then to hinder these men from depressing or inflating the value of all kinds of property to suit their caprice or avarice, and thereby gathering into their own coffers the wealth of the nation? Where is the limit to such a power as this? What shall be said of the spirit of a few people who will submit without a protest to be thus bound hand and foot? I have hinted at some of the dangers which menace our future. If it be to correct these evils, and to avert these dangers your League has been organized, it will receive the benedictions of the people.

The practical question is, "What are you going to do about it?" To my mind the answer is easy. This organized gigantic corporate power can only be kept under proper restraint by the organized power of the people, expressed through their State and National Governments. That such governmental power exists and may properly be exercised I have not a particle of doubt. It is plainly written in our constitutions, and has been unequivocally declared by the Supreme Court of the United States.

The limits of this letter will not permit a discussion of the constitutional question nor a detailed statement of the practical remedy for existing evil. I may, however, venture to suggest that, in my judgment, the first and most important duty of Congress is to emancipate the people from the supervision and control of corporate monopoly, by the establishment of a system of postal telegraphy, whereby they shall be afforded a safe, sure and cheap method of communication with each other. There is no doubt of the economy and success of such a system. It has been tried in other countries with most satisfactory results.

I am aware that it will require much care, labor and skill to frame laws which shall successfully regulate and restrain the action of the great transportation companies, without unnecessary injury to them, and without omitting the essential elements of protection to the public, but I have no doubt it can be done. When the people demand it they will find the men to do it. I believe the time has come when this great work should be undertaken.

It will be far better for the corporations themselves that it be done now, by conservative but thorough and judicious legislation, rather than to postpone it until the people, no longer able to bear the tyranny of corporate power, shall rise in their wrath to humble and destroy their oppressors. At some convenient time I shall endeavor to state specifically some of the legislative remedies I would propose.

Excuse the great length of this letter, and believe me, very sincerely your friend,   WILLIAM WINDOM.

NEW YORK, February 21.—A large mass-meeting was held to-night at Cooper Institute under the auspices of the National Anti-Monopoly League. Peter Cooper was present. President L. E. Chittenden briefly stated the objects and purposes of the league, asserting its origin to be the outgrowth of the abuses of corporate powers, and urging the necessity of universal organization on some systematic basis by the entire tax-paying element of the country.

Judge Black, of Pennsylvania, was introduced. He spoke for over an hour, and in the course of his address, of which the key-note was the legal and constitutional aspects of the transportation question, considered at length the relations of corporations to the public. He said that the course of these institutions had been steadily towards complete monopoly; that their ultimate designs were fraught with the greatest danger to the State, and that unless legislation should step in and aid the oppressed people the whole machinery of the government would be thrown into the hands of monopolists. "These men," said the speaker, " are not now satisfied with their possessions; they will still continue to water their stocks, to absorb the property of others, and to tax the producers at their own caprice, and by the consolidation of railroads, union of telegraph lines, subversion of laws, and insecurity given corporate properties by their refusal to recognize the rights of minority shareholders they have the rights of the public and individual, prevented beneficial competition, and trampled upon the spirit of the constitution and laws of their country."

He advocated that railroad men should be turned out of office under the government and their duties compelled, as well as rights observed, through the interposition of law. The constitutional methods by which the people might be protected in their rights were discussed and authorities quoted to demonstrate that the remedy lay in the hands of the public itself. It was shown that by the power of their wealth railroads had obtained a large share of the control of Supreme and State courts and various legislative bodies, and that judges were elected and representatives selected with special reference to their fitness for advancing the interests of the corporations they represented. The railroads were rapidly assuming an influence disproportionate to the relative position they occupied toward other bodies. The character and intent of such laws as should be enacted was explained, and their adoption strongly recommended.

The speaker was frequently interrupted by applause, and at one time when he asked the question, "What shall we do with these corporations?" a man in the audience shouted: "Confiscate their stealings." "Well," was the answer, "we would like to, but they've carried them out of sight."

United States Senator Windom sent a letter. After stating the

to banish from the councils all communistic spirit and recognize the force of power against which it had to contend, Senator Windom treated at length of the abuses which exist in the management of the railroads and telegraphs, and laid much stress on the danger of a single man controlling the educational power of the press by the ownership of telegraphs, and strongly advocated a postal telegraph and governmental restraint to be exercised over the increase of corporate powers. "Without such restraint," the letter reads "what is to fix the limit to the exactions of the corporate power upon the people? What is there to hinder these men from depressing or inflating the value of all kinds of property to suit their caprice or avarice? What shall be said of a free people who will submit without protest to be bound hand and foot?"

"I have hinted at some of the dangers which menace our future. If it be to correct these evils and avert these dangers your league has been organized, it will receive the benedictions of the people."

In conclusion it was suggested that such laws be framed as would regulate and restrain the action of the great transportation companies without unnecessary injury to them, and without omitting the essential elements of protection to the public.

The meeting was next addressed by Congressman Reagan, who addressed himself principally to the practical remedies which had been proposed for the abuses of corporate powers, and explained the features of the Reagan bill, recently introduced into Congress for the regulation of interstate commerce by railroads, as a step in the right direction. The following resolution was then introduced :

Resolved, That it is the duty of citizens everywhere to organize anti-monopoly leagues, and endeavor to secure, among others, the following specific results:

First—Laws compelling the transportation and telegraph companies to base their charges on risk and cost of service.

Second—Laws to prevent the pooling of combinations.

Third—Laws to prevent discriminations against any class of citizens on public highways.

Fourth—Courts to give effect to the laws placed on the statute books.

Fifth—Laws to make it the official duties of officers to defend citizens against corporate injustice.

Ssixth—Laws to prevent public taxation to pay dividends on national stocks.

Seventh—Laws against bribery.

Eighth—Laws to regulate the commerce of the several States.

Ninth—A liberal policy towards water-ways.

It was resolved that independent journals should be encouraged, and that the bread, meat, and fuel of the masses should not be taxed to pay dividends on fictitious costs of construction.

The meeting was afterwards addressed by others advocating the principles embodied in the resolutions, which were adopted.

APPENDIX "J."

Villard's Railroad and Steamship Lines.

How the Anaconda Coils Around the New States and Territories.

WALLA WALLA, W. T., July 13.—There is no part of the United States more heartily opposed to monopolies than this, and for the very good reason that there is no part of the United States more tortured by the modern rack, monopoly.

The device which, screw-like, keeps the current of financial life from healthy coursing through the veins of this member of that body politic, is the most powerful of all the engines for subduing and crushing peoples, without resistance—railroads.

About two years ago Mr. Henry Villard, and Eastern capitalists whom he represented, purchased of some gentlemen, mostly residing in Portland, Oregon, the chief stock of the Oregon Steamship and Navigation Company. This company carried passengers and freight by steamers from and to Portland, and up and down the Columbia and Snake Rivers, going as far east as Wallula, Washington Territory, and Lewiston, Idaho Territory, and from Wallula, by railroad thirty miles, to Walla Walla.' Since obtaining control of this property he has constructed a broad-gauge railroad from Wallula, along the south bank of the Columbia River, to The Dalles, Oregon, and intends to continue it to Portland. To this line he has built five or six feeders, running a distance of thirty to sixty miles in a northeasterly direction from Walla Walla, and southeasterly from the Columbia River into Eastern Oregon. As is well known he has also recently obtained control of the land-grant privileges and property of the Northern Pacific Railway. The land-grant of the Northern Pacific in this territory takes every other section of seven-eighths of the tillable land; in Oregon, every other section along the northern boundary east of the Cascade Mountains for a width of twenty miles. Its privileges, the right of way, its property, a railroad nearly completed from Ainsworth, at the mouth of Snake River, to Spokan Falls, 149 miles, and about 160 miles of railroad in operation on the western side of the territory, together with some rolling-stock, docks, houses, etc. Since obtaining control of the Northern Pacific Railroad he has bought the "Star" line of steamers, running on the western coast of the territory, and has obtained control of the "Oregon Railway Company, Limited," which has narrow-gauge lines running in various directions, so as to pretty thoroughly tap the north three-quarters of Western Oregon. Before buying and building these various railroad and steamship lines, he, as representative, owned or controlled the old Ben Holladay property, a line of ocean steamships plying between Portland and San Francisco, and the "Oregon & California Railroad," running directly south through Western Oregon, from Portland to Roseburgh, a distance of 200 miles.

To summarize, it can be briefly said that he owns or controls about half the realty in this territory and a big slice of Oregon; that he owns and controls all the railroads in Washington Territory and Oregon, and every steamboat line in their interior, and substantially the steamships of their coasts.

Of course the object Mr. Villard had in buying, leasing, and building, was to shut down on all manner of competition that he might become extortionate. I will illustrate: Oregon Railway & Navigation Company freight rates from Walla Walla to Portland, 270 miles—Wheat, 24 cents a bushel, not including wharfage, loading cars, etc.; wool in sacks and dry hides, 1¼ cents a pound. From Portland to Walla Walla, first-class freight, as farm machinery and furniture, 17 mills a pound; second-class, 1½ cents a pound; third-class, 1¼ cents; fourth-class, 1⅛ cents. Any freight of less weight than 100 pounds charged as though it were 100.

·The rates over any of the Villard lines in Eastern Oregon and Washington Territory are equally oppressive. Those in Western Oregon and Washington I am unacquainted with, but I have no reason for thinking they are less extortionate.

The rate of freight on grain from Chicago to New York, 979 miles, in the winter when there is no lake competition, is 30 to 35 cents a hundred pounds, other freight relatively. The rate on a ton of second-class from Portland to Walla Walla, 270 miles, is 30; from San Francisco to Portland, 730 miles, $4; from China to Frisco, $2.50.

Men who are competent to judge, through the experience of travel over the entire west, pronounce this country, east of the Cascade range, one of the best for a farmer. Most of the soil is exceedingly prolific in small grains, and easily cultivated. Part of the labor of the six creative days was well put in here. All that is needed to make it rarely prosperous is competitive freights to tidewater. For nearly fifteen years the people of this country have been looking forward to the completion of the Northern Pacific Railroad. During the last year, up to three months ago, promises, and better still, signs were given, which made the people confident of an immediate construction of the Northern Pacific Railroad from here to Puget Sound. Such a road meant competition—that is to say reasonable freights. About three months ago, as has been said, Mr V...ard secured control of the Northern Pacific Railroad, which meant no competition—that is to say, exorbitant freights. But beyond that it destroyed hope, so difficult of separation from the future. There are but three passes for railroads from this section to the Pacific Ocean, one over the Cascade Mountains, the other two the north and south bank of the Columbia River. Henry Villard now holds them all.—*Cincinnati Gazette.*

The Value of the Land Grant.

The value of the land grant of the Northern Pacific is greater than is usually known. While the times forbade the rapid completion of the road, and the limit had been passed which its charter allowed for building, its managers did not think it wise to boast of the value of their franchise in the face of a Congress that had already raised the question of a forfeiture. Since money has come into the treasury by the bushel to finish the road, and the Secretary of the Interior has decided that the charter of the Northern Pacific, unlike the charters of most land grant roads, does not permit of a forfeiture, this reserve about the land grant has worn off. Where it runs through a State, the Northern Pacific has half the land—distributed in alternate sections—for twenty miles on each side of its track. In other words, it has the equivalent of a solid strip twenty miles wide through Wisconsin, west of Montreal River, and through Minnesota. Through Dakota, Montana, Idaho, and along the Cascade Branch, it has what is equal to a solid strip of land forty miles wide.

If its other branch on the Pacific slope runs between Oregon and Washington, it will have beside the above the half of a strip forty miles wide in Washington, and half of one twenty miles wide in Oregon. Its charter gives it a double line, and so a double land grant, on the Pacific Coast. So, when the Northern Pacific buys the Oregon Railway & Navigation Company's line, it will take with it a land grant of immense value. It may do this, for its charter permits it expressly to build or acquire in order to complete its line from the lakes to the Pacific. Its main line and its branches will give the Northern Pacific on the Pacific Coast an equivalent of a belt seventy miles wide to tide water.

But this is not all, as much of the land that lay in the path of the Northern Pacific had been taken up, or would be taken up before its grant occurred, by pre-emptions, homesteads, by grants to other railroads, by reservations to Indians and similar causes. Congress provided that when such shortages occurred the road could take an equivalent amount of land anywhere within a belt ten miles wide on each side of its original land grant. And, still later, Congress gave it permission to recoup itself from any such shortages that were made after 1864, by taking an equal amount of land out of a second indemnity belt ten miles wide on each side of the first indemnity limit. That is, the Northern Pacific takes, with the exception of what the Government has already disposed of, one-half of a belt forty miles wide through Wisconsin, forty miles wide through Minnesota, eighty miles wide through Dakota, eighty miles wide through Montana, eighty miles wide through Idaho, eighty miles wide through Washington along the Cascade Branch, forty miles wide along the Portland Branch in Washington, and twenty miles wide in Oregon along the last named branch. Then if it finds itself short say, for illustration, 5,000,000 acres of the amount of land it ought to have, it may recoup itself to that amount out of any unappropriated land within the two indemnity belts. These give it an additional strip forty miles wide from the lakes to the Pacific within which to make its selection. It may take up all its shortage at any point in this belt where it finds the most valuable land. If the best land, for instance, lay in Montana the road could make up all its shortage there, and might take one-half of all the land for a width of 120 miles until its land grant was satisfied.—*Chicago Tribune, July 22.*

Gold, Silver, and Paper Money in Circulation in Twenty-four Countries.

We give the estimated amount of gold and silver and paper money in circulation in twenty-four countries at the latest dates:

	Paper Money.	Specie — Total gold and silver.
Austria...	$322,938,854	$ 70,560,000
Australia...	21,604,936	50,000,000
Belgium..	58,419,000	174,000,000
Brazil	91,000,000	Nominal.
Canada...	29,047,000	10,291,285
Colombia...	1,895,343	4,700,000
Denmark...	18,900,000	28,863,000
France...	466,755,000	1,159,244,850
Germany...	229,596,220	543,108,419
Great Britain.......................................	200,148,875	711,995,211
Greece...	12,890,000	7,500,000
Italy	135,000,000	40,000,000
Japan..	143,000,000	50,000,000
Mexico...	1,500,000	77,980,000
Netherlands..	73,233,000	11,200,000
Norway..	10,300,000	1,882,000
Peru...	13,038,820	85,000,000
Portugal	29,520,000	110,000,000
Russia...	587,907,000	200,000,000
Spain..	33,795,000	18,120,000
Sweden..	11,680,000	94,700,000
Turkey..	100,000,000	Nominal.
United States, 1879................................	683,943,799	427,206,852
	$3,306,480,151	$3,900,851,635

—Indianapolis Journal, June 25th.

Local Debts.

OUR DEBTS.

The census returns of indebtedness shows that the aggregate debts of
311 cities in the United States having a population of 7,500 and over are
$710,535,000, of which $682,096,000 is bonded and $28,439,000 floating.
The same cities have an aggregate of $117,191,000 sinking funds, so that
their net debts are $593,344,000. The aggregate debts of the States are
estimated at $250,000,000, and the aggregate debts of towns, townships,
and school districts are estimated at $225,000,000. This would make the
aggregate debts of all kinds except the national debt $1,069,076,000.